The Symphony of Life

by

Lee R. Madden

DORRANCE
PUBLISHING CO
EST. 1920
PITTSBURGH, PENNSYLVANIA 15238

Dorrance Publishing Co
585 Alpha Drive
Suite 103
Pittsburgh, PA 15238
Visit our website at *www.dorrancebookstore.com*

ISBN: 978-1-4809-1806-2
eISBN: 978-1-4809-1726-3

Lord Our Eyes Grow Dim

Oh! Lord our eyes grow dim

Their thunder sounds muffled to our ears

The days seem long

The nights even longer

We long for our loved ones

You now hold in Your loving arms

We know our time seems near

Yet we know not the tasks

We must complete

Amen

I dedicate this story to all the staff of the McCrite Plaza Retirement Community, for their enjoyment. It is you who contribute a part of your energy and self-confidence and loyalty to the care of the elderly and those in need of special care, and still return to your own families with a smile on your face, help a child with home-work, eat supper, watch TV, then off to sleep. It is my opinion that not all the angels abide in heaven!

We must give special accolades to Marge, the beautician whose clients leave her shop looking and feeling like beauty queens, ready for church, or our many special holidays, greet family, or elevate a dour mood.

An accolade to the van driver who carries us to our various doctor appointments and on tours about the city and nearby towns when we are feeling well again… and to the outside maintenance people who keep the lawn and fountain clear and sparkling and clear the windblown trash that might accumulate.

All of your efforts do not go unnoticed by our friends, families, or mentors who think and say, "These people really care about the welfare of the residents."

List of Characters

Anonymous auto-transport driver

Jim Smith- Owner of Smith Auto Agency; left arm was injured in a farm accident. Father of John. Both men are community boosters.

John Smith- Age twenty; son of Jim.

Eva (Ma) and Jake (Pa) Smith- Grandparents of John Smith.

Erma- Temporary secretary of Smith Auto Agency; fiancé of John.

"Valree"- Chet's little sister (page 95).

"Chet" Chester Curtis- First year college student. Has grain truck, "-I Will Help You Harvest." Wants to finish school; interested in co-operative management.

"Chess" Wilson- A trusted friend and farm manager for the Jake (PA) Smith Farms

Albert and Sarah Goldsmith- Owners of the Bar Z Cattle and Wheat Ranch, north of Stockton, Kansas.

Joyce and Tamala Goldsmith- Daughters working as waitress at Stockman's Café; hope to start nurse training.

D. Andrew Webber- Chief of surgery, McCook Hospital.

Mrs. Clara North- Director of Volunteer McCook Hospital.

Dr. Sam Wilson- The other half of the Webber and Wilson surgery team.

McCook Nebraska Hospital- An accredited hospital.

Bobby-The cleft lip and palate baby boy (Webber and J).

Jacson- The burned baby boy (Webber and J).

Ella- The under-nourished baby (Webber and J).

Elmer- A youth with a broken leg (Wilson and T).

Petty- A boy suspected of having hepatitis A (Wilson and T).

Psychologists- Dr. Blue and wife, Fay.

Dr. Paggett- Plastic surgeon.

Mrs. Elva Brandon- Little Eve's Mother.

Mr. Don Claskie and wife, "Dora- The mail restaurant owners.

Ray Albertson and wife, Evelan.

Ray is a builder of large commercial structures while Evelan is a church and community leader who wants her husband to retire before the family is scattered to the four winds.

Joy Albertson- Eldest son of Ray and Evelan following in the footsteps of his father.

Tim Albertson- Ray and Evelan's youngest son. Hopes to become a doctor; worries about his father not spending more time at home.

Avery Graham- Pilot for Albertson company. Also does ferrying for other companies.

Annabell Graham- Wife of Avery Graham, slightly younger than he. Feels she is becoming weary of their nomadic life. Very good friend of Evelan Albertson; she feels their lives are lonely- more so perhaps because Annabell does not appear as devout. We have a feeling that is about to change.

Hap and Marion- Owners of the Lonesome Pine Cage in Paradise Village.

Dr. Will Grover- Administrator- elect of the ICU; has a disabling stroke.

Dr. Annata Quinn- A charming, skilled physician chosen to replace Dr. Will Grover.

Mr. Dan McCarthy- Nebraska detective called in by Dr. John Smith for a mysterious problem.

Reminiscence of a 1960 Model Auto

by Lee R. Madden

I remember sitting shackled in the huge transporter, waiting to be unloaded with my load-mates; we were to be left at the very large show-lot of an Auto dealer at the outskirts of a large city in Kansas. The very center, they had told me as they were unloaded of the United States of America. I can see then, even today, as they all were lined up under the string of bright lights and flapping pennants, I wanted so very much to join them, as I thought of all the exciting people they would meet and who their owners would be.

My thoughts and desires turned to dismay as the driver and his helper started driving out of the lot. I tugged at my shackles and even tried to sound my beautiful musical horn, but my restraints held me tight. The driver soon turned to the right into a narrow dirt road line with yellow, waving wheat. In the fields were large harvesting machines. In some fields were several machines following obliquely behind the leader. Each machine had an attendant truck into which bushels and bushels of wheat were pouring. As we progressed toward our destination, the road was undulated with empty trucks returning from the large elevators we had seen near the railroad. Soon, there were loud air horns behind us.

My driver looked back and there was a string of heavy loaded wheat trucks that were unable to pass us as the "empty" had. The only solution to the dilemma seemed that my driver must increase his speed to exceed that of the loaded trucks, until a pass could be negotiated. With the increased speed, we soon outdistanced the heavily loaded trucks.

The dust was stifling and drifting all over my beautiful silver grey upholstery. We continued at this reckless speed to our destination, a small, quiet farm village, set in an enchanting paradise of shady green lawns and fresh-painted older homes and surrounded by fields of ripening golden wheat.

I was unceremoniously offloaded by the driver and his helper, assistant mechanic of the local auto agency. There I sat, contemplating my miserable appearance. Dust everywhere and no wheel-covers on my naked wheels. Soon, a group of men and boys gathered about me, I was so embarrassed when a husky young man strolled over and softly wiped the dust from my head-lamps, and asked me if I was interested in finding a new home. Then, in a soft voice, he began speaking of his mother and father and that he wanted to start agricultural college that fall and about someone… he called "Erma," his voice wistfully trailed off-.

Quickly, he changed the subject and said, "Let's get you into the 'beauty shop' I know that a trip through the 'No Scratches' automatic wash will make all the difference in your outlook on life. Then, we will put your wheel-covers on when the mechanics in the shop check your 'vitals.' As I started to shower, I began to have my doubts about this brash young man! I was not to see him for a week. How was I to know that he might have been one of those drivers that had "honked" us into town just hours ago?

After all that waxing, primping, and tinkering by the mechanic and his helpers, I was driven into the show-room. There, I was my reflection in the display window. Long "extra length estate body" Aqua Blue with five doors and five rows of bench seats and a narrow walk-way down the center with lights over each. Air, heat vents at floor level and fans directed toward each window fastened to the ceiling to prevent "window fog" completed the entities.

My week in the display-room was an introduction to the village of Paradise city and the people who called it home. My first visitor, of course, was Jim Smith, the owner of the auto agency, who confided that I was special and to remain until the next Sunday, as most of the farm people would be in on Saturday night. I also over-heard him ask the secretary to be sure all the papers were in son John's name and to be sure that the license plate was installed by the shop, as Sunday would be John's birthday.

I soon learned that Secretary "Erma" was just temporary for the summer, as the other girl was in the hospital with twin girls. She had asked for a leave to adjust to the increase in her family. I also now understood the wistfulness in John's voice the day I arrived in Paradise. I noticed that Jim Smith had injured his left hand when he was quite young, helping his father grind ear-corn for winter feed for his cattle on their farm. Jim had always dreamed of going to medical school, but that had disappeared after the injury. Jim found that he had a talent in sales and was soon selling autos and truck for the agency. Jim had bought the agency when the owner retired.

In the passing years, John was drawn to the farm of his grandparents. He and Erma had spent many days helping his grandparents with the more difficult tasks when time of the elements was against them completing the tasks.

Well, here it is, Saturday morning and visitors were beginning to drift into the display-room, but nowhere was John; it had been three long days since he came in. Erma came out of the office grumbling about "Get used to is, as it happens every harvest," then went back to answer the phone.

It would be three more days before I was to see John more disheveled and weary, young many I had ever seen, walked in to the showroom of the Ford agency where I had been on display. When John started to speak, I knew this was the birthday boy that "Erma" had been talking about...

John began telling me he had been helping his grandparents harvest their wheat crop as the "window" of good weather was drawing to a close. John began by saying his grandfather had tried to cut the first round of the "back swath, but had not the strength to maneuver the combine from an abandon electric fence post, resulting in damage to a replaceable section of the cycle-bar. And how his grandfather had removed the cycle-bar by the time John arrived, and in the process had received a gash across the palm of his left hand. Although the cut was not too serious, it did need attention and a tetanus shot. After stopping to pick up his grandfather, who with a "What is next, Pa?" and all the while he kept saying it was just retribution for the time forty years ago when Jim caught his hand in that feed grinder. Here wrap your hand in this towel and get in the car and John will drive us to the doctor in Paradise City.

Arriving at the doctor's office in Paradise City, John ushered his grandparents into the office where the doctor and nurse was waiting for then. The wound was quickly cleansed and disinfected, and bandaged. The doctor, knowing the elderly man's aversion to "shots," had quietly instructed the nurse to prepare the syringe. He would distract the patient. In a flash, the crisis was over.

Turning to John, the doctor said, "The wound will be quite painful for several days. We will give him a pain tablet now. He should take it on every three hours for the next twenty-four. After that, we should be able to spread them every six hours."

Saga of a 1960 Auto

Grandfather Smith had returned to the farm home after leaving the doctor's office. Grandfather and John carefully laid him on the bed, his head slightly raised, his left arm resting on a soft pillow, raised just enough to prevent the blood "pooling" in the veins. "Pa" was protesting, saying, "he was being treated like a child." In a short time, he relaxed and drifted off to sleep, just as the doctor had planned.

In the meantime, John cleaned up the mess in the kitchen and started the washing machine and even washed all the bedclothes for every bed in the house and the clothes-dryer running. Grandmother Smith had taken a fat rooster from the freezer and defrosted it in the microwave. She returned to check on "Pa." She had sat down "for just a minute" when she fell asleep.

John put the fat chicken on to boil so that Grandpa would have plenty of broth and plenty of pureed meat for the next day or so.

"Chet" Curtis was a college student from the capital of Kansas where his parents lived. He had planned all winter on making the harvest this year, to earn enough to start medical school. Even his five-year-old sister had given him a dollar from her piggy-bank "to buy a grain truck." With his saving, he had made a payment on a used Ford one and a half-ton with good tires and a spare. He had stopped for gas at The SMITH AUTO AGENCY and saw the unique van in the showroom. "Erma" was just leaving when "Chet" asked her where he could find some work, saying, "Have truck, will haul." Erma was quick to tell him about her fiancé's grandfather had injured his left hand and "I know he could use some help.

5

"I am going out to the home right now to "spell" Granny Smith, bless her, she will be down too, just from worry. Follow me, it is only a mile north of town on the black top county road."

On arrival, they found Grandpa Smith sitting at the kitchen table, his left arm stretched out horizontally. He had just taken his first pain medication and was resting comfortably. He was not doing too bad with a large bowl of hot pureed chicken mixed with little hot broth, at feeding himself.

Erma introduced Chet, saying, "He would like to help us harvest. He says he has never made the harvest before, but with your wisdom and his brawn, I'll bet we will get the wheat to the market."

Grandpa Smith turned to Erma and said, "It is time, Ma, and I retired and moved into town. We will turn the farm over to John and you."

Erma reminded him that John wanted to start medical school this fall and to start nurse training also. Even Chet intends to be a doctor. "Wait until after harvest and if you find a nice house in Paradise City, we will talk about it again."

That night, John Smith and Chet Curtis shared a room on the third floor of the rambling old farm house. They had talked late into the night and a plan was beginning to crystallize in his mind. He and Chet would work the harvest and store all the wheat at the co-op elevator and work the ground and plan the winter wheat as a cash-crop.

"Then, if Grandpa wanted to keep raising his pure bred heifers, we could plant some mil and some alfalfa. Then we could go to school and hire a customer-cutter if we had to. We need a full time man with him with the cattle, because that is a year-round job."

John and Chet were awake at dawn. They explained they should not begin cutting wheat for at least a couple of hours, because in this part of the state, there is always a lot of moisture in the air over-night, and standing wheat absorbs enough to be docked a penny and bushel at the CO-OP ELEVATOR. We generally have a breeze about sun up, and it evaporates most of the moisture in about two hours. We will have time to get the chores done and eat a good breakfast, too.

We will start the windmill and pump a tank of water for the stock, put out some ensilage for the cattle, milk the ten cows and start the cream-separator. Then, we will eat breakfast.

Chet remarked, "I always thought milk came in cartons at the grocery store! You mean to tell me Grandpa has been doing this for forty years?"

"Oh, it could get worse if we should have a breakdown," John replied with a grin.

After they had eaten breakfast, John asked Chet to gas up the combine, both trucks, and Grandpa's ton pick-up, which had a lot of tools in it, so if we have trouble with the combine, Grandma will bring the truck to us.

Erma will take the first load in-to town and drop off the Smith grub box at the café. They will have it ready to come back at twelve noon with the ten-gallon cooler of lemonade. There is a five-gallon cooler of water in each truck and combine also.

"If either truck should be stuck in a clogged unloading line at the elevator, just use your cell phone and call grandma and she will come in with her little pick-up and take that driver his lunch and bring us ours." [nbbande3]

There is an unwritten code that a driver must stay with his truck in line at all times, and move forward when the lead trucks moves into the elevator.

Saga of Paradise Village and the

Cooperative Enterprises

Grandma Smith had somehow managed to take Grandpa into town every morning to have the nurse and doctor redress the wound. The rain had allowed Erma and Grandma an extra hour of rest. As they drove up to the doctor's office, the town was alive with idled harvesters. After the hand had been cleansed and redressed the doctor gave him some antibiotic tablets to be taken one a day.

"We had better dress the hand every day for at least another week," the doctor said, adding, "The wound is doing nicely. We just do not want to take any chances with out senior citizens."

When they returned to the farmland, the elderly couple retired to the living room and their easy chairs. Pa listened to the radio for weather and wheat prices. Ma watched *The Farm Woman of Today* show on TV.

Erma went to see how the two girls were doing with the housework and if anything was needed to be brought from the grocery store.

Pa, listening to the cattle markets, knew he had seven prime steers ready for market. He walked into an adjoining room where John Smith had posted a plaque, PA SMITH'S FARM OFFICE, some ten years ago in celebration of his seventy-fifth birthday. It had contained a large desk and an even larger table with mountains of hand-written farm records dating back to the year he had taken over the operation of the farm from his elderly father. A year later, he and Ma were married, as Ma's fine Spenserian penmanship began to appear on the records. After placing the plaque that day, John and Erma vowed they would move every record on a huge computer they had urged Pa to buy.

This morning, as Pa entered the room, it was as if he were in the office of his co-op elevator office, to call the rand hand on the cell phone to start loading the seven steers in the one and a half-ton pick-up with the short cattle trailer. After all, the seven steers would weigh at least 5,600 pounds, he estimated and the truck had a sleeper cab, too. The huge Kenilworth Diesel with the huge sleeper cab, with short wave radio cover that could be used for long haul to Houston, Texas, if the rail should be glutted with grain.

After making sure Ches Wilson would have the rig ready to pull out by ten AM, Pa went in to ask Ma to adjust the sling and place a small plastic bag with a row of small ventilator holes over his hand. He also asked her to go with him to Stockton, saying, "We can get $1000.00 a head for prime today, if we can get there by noon. Maybe! We will eat at the Stockman's café when we get unloaded."

After unloading the cattle in Stockton, Kansas, the three parked in the café's TRUCK PARKING special for long trucks, just pulling in between the long slanted yellow lines that were wide enough apart the truck doors opened easily. Later, one could just pull forward directly into a one-way drive that led to another driveway, this one leading to the high-way with traffic going the same way one wished to go, no backing required, and visibly good.

When the three entered the air-conditioned STOCKMAN'S CAFÉ, they were greeted by their many farm friends, many as elderly as Pa and Ma Smith. They were all solicitous about Pa's wound and how soon he would be able to feed himself, with Ms fielding most of the questions with a flipped remark.

A Waitress came and whispered in ma's ear that her elderly parents, Albert and Sarah, owners of the Bar K Ranch, were waiting in the big book number 10 in quiet corner, for them to come and lunch with them. Ma turned abruptly to Pa and said "Pa, Albert and Sarah Goldsmith are waiting over in both ten to each lunch with us. Let us go now!" As they neared the booth, the expression on Sarah's face was that of terrific pain., Rushing over to Sarah, Ma exclaimed, "Oh Sarah whatever is the matter?"

"I think it is my heart" she whispered. "It really hurts and I am so dizzy, too."

Ma reached in her hand-bag for the cell phone and called 911 and asked for a ground and air ambulance. Someone had alerted the local doctor, who just happened to be in the next block and listening to the chatter on the radio. He was at the café in one minute, air horn blowing wildly. He stabilized the patient by the time the ambulances arrived. Dr. Scott made arrangements with the McCook Nebraska hospital for her care.

In the meantime, Sarah had been loaded in the copter and the pilot talking to emergency at McCook, on his radio, that his arrival would be one PM. By the time he finished talking, the copter was 500 feet in the air and rising another 1000 feet and on a direct course with the hospital. He would also have the co-pilot transmit the vital statistics, so those waiting at the emergency would know how to proceed when the copter arrived.

Upon arrival at the McCook hospital, the leader of the emergency team and two nurses rechecked the vitals to make sure Mrs. Sarah Goldsmith had remained stabilized during the flight and checked the IV fluids, to avoid any conflict should more be needed, and attached the oxygen, while others were applying the EKG sensor pads and automatic pressure cuff. The x-rays, the blood samples were being checked in the lab.

Joyce, the waitress, had ridden with the air ambulance, tucked into an alcove of the copter, watching the emergency crew as they responded to every situation as it arose. Joyce and Tamala Goldsmith had been working at the Stockman's Café that summer after graduating from high school. Both planned to start nurses training in the fall.

Joyce had just spent the last half hour talking to the hospital administrator, who was trying to establish a health record, when a nurse contacted her that her mother was being prepared for surgery and needed a consent form filled out. The nurse assured her that this type of surgery was now being performed routinely. The nurse and the doctor had explained the operation to Joyce while the x-rays were being taken and was now "scrubbing-up" or he would explain the procedure himself again.

The administrator explained he had looked at the x-rays with the doctors and had all concluded that cholesterol was found in the blood test.

The x-rays show in blocking some blood to the brain. That accounts for your mother's dizziness. We concluded that so far, there is very little damage to the heart itself. We can thank the quick action of Mrs. Smith and her cell phone and ambulance crew with the oxygen for no damage to the brain. We may be able to dissolve the cholesterol with drugs and proper diet. I think the surgery is over by now; however, the surgeons will not close until they are sure there are no leaks. You know that the arteries of the elderly are not as elastic as in their youth. Be assured that every patient is given very good care in this hospital. The heroic starts when we are unable to see the patient promptly. Our emergency people have a motto. "Time means life." I shall call and aid to take you down to a nourishing meal and a nurse will lay you down to a nourishing meal and a nurse will take you to your mother and explain why she is sedated and in intensive care and how soon into a room," the administrator said.

A lady in a pink uniform appeared at the door of the administrator's door and was introduced as Mrs. "Clara" North.

"She is the leader of our volunteer group that assists the families of our patients in finding their way around our large hospital. She will take dinner with you this evening and show you where the chapel is located," said the administrator.

Clara said, "I'll bet you haven't eaten since late this morning, have you? Let us start with a clear broth, quite warm, followed by a small side dish, pureed blanched carrots, and a small, very lean steak with almost no salt. That should all be easy to digest this late in the afternoon. Now, we need a sweet tangy fruit, like a small fresh peach and a few concord grapes, and a second cup of tea."

They ate leisurely. Clara began to talk to Joyce.

"When you first see your mother, she may appear disoriented as she recovers from the anesthetic, but that will pass quickly. The surgeon cleared the blockage from the artery where it separates, to carry blood, under the left or right ear, to the brain, and the other to the scalp. In mild cases, it is done very quickly, to avoid depriving the brain of blood. Your mother is very lucky to have a friend like Mrs. Smith, who called for help quickly."

They stopped at the chapel for a brief prayer, then on to the recovery room to see her mother, where neither would really remember what was said. Later that night, Joyce called home to tell her father and Mr. and Mrs. Smith that everything went fine and everyone at the hospital had been very kind. She said she should be able to have visitors by Sunday.

"Don't try to drive. Have Tamala drive you all up," Joyce commanded in a quavering voice.

Joyce, after the brief visit with her mother in the recovery room, had called her father in Stockton and assured him that her mother was recovering quite well and to pass the word to all at the Stockman's café when down for a coffee the next morning.

Hanging up the phone, Joyce went directly to the chapel and poured out her heart in gratefulness that her mother's crisis had passed, vowing that she would be in the first enrollment for nurse training that fall.

Arising from her knees, she walked back to the recovery room, informing the nurse at the desk that she would be in room 202, assigned to her mother when she would be released form recovery sometime in the morning.

On entering the room, she saw it had all the amenities of any regular hospital room with one exception: It had a nice well-furnished sitting room, a desk, well-lighted, two easy chairs, a floor-lamp or two, and a lounge all ready made up as a bed for her! "How thoughtful," she said under her breath. Over in a corner was a tiny rocker for a child. Tossing of her shoes, lay down and was soon in the land of Nod, only to awaken when Clara entered the next morning with a tray of coffee and toast.

As they sipped their coffee, Clara brought Joyce up about the progress of her mother. She explained blood tests had been made twice during the night that showed that the blood thinner was doing the job of lowering her blood pressure and a strange-sounding medicine was helping reduce the cholesterol, though she will have to reduce to a minimum fatty foods in the diet.

"It is time we went down to see your mother. The doctors have planned for her to sit up about half an hour this morning and in a chair this afternoon if she got along all right this morning."

At the beginning pages of this narrative, we listened to the woes of a discouraged, specially built 1960 model, low, stretched-out, Ford V8 passenger van that Mr. Jim Smith had ordered for his son's birthday. Hopefully, his son, John, would become a great medical doctor and sugeon. Knowing his own injury in his youth had disrupted his own dream.

Now, with the wheat harvest almost over at the Smith Farm, John Smith decided it was the ideal time to "open" his birthday present. He and Erma visited the auto agency and asked his father if his mechanic and helper would be free to drive them to the McCook hospital, stopping at Stockman's Café for lunch, and picking up Mr. Albert Goldsmith and his other daughter, Tamala, and of course, my grandma, who just had to stay with Tamala. Grandpa has been calling her every morning to hear how she was feeling.

"We would like to leave about one PM Saturday and be back sometime Monday. I just feel better with a professional driver on a long fast trip," John remarked.

"How could I resist such a humanitarian request?" replied Jim Smith. "If need be, my parts manager can fill in as mechanic a day or so and we will learn how much his helper has learned, too. Oh! By the way, the repair-rebuild department added a small comfort room in the van, their contribution to the elderly. The whole town is expecting great things that will be of benefit the whole village."

The van and drivers were waiting at the door and had given a walkthrough of the van. An hour later, they were parked in the easy-park stalls at the Stock man's café. After a quick lunch, they had another walk-through of nearly an hour because everyone in the café had asked to see the "luxury liner."

The mechanic and his helper were showing a group of mid-aged men to the V8 diesel engine with the four-speed automatic transmission that "worked smooth as glad." John called to them that they were due in McCook by three PM.

Pulling out of the parking, the driver went straight into a drive that had an arrow pointing North, leading easily into the fast moving traffic.

Arriving at the hospital, the group was shown to room 202. Sarah Goldsmith had been walking twice a day the past two days, supported on the arms of two husky therapists who reported that Mrs. Goldsmith was gaining strength every day.

"But we need to keep her on a regular routine and not one where she has been riding a horse and herding cattle! Like she says she has been doing all her life!" they said.

Tamala stepped over to where her mother was resting.

"They are just trying to keep you here because you are so easy to care for. We will invite them to the ranch for a barbecue some time!"

The bantering went on a few minutes. Albert Goldsmith entered the room, his expensive tailored business suit, soft leather high-heeled custom-made boots, black string tie, brocaded white shirt, indicating his many years in the ranch and cattle business. He had just talked to the doctor who had advised him that he took should have a full physical check-up. Sarah was recovering well, but the doctor had suggested "a little more time with the therapist and we learn more about these special diets we hope will help thousands of people in this world."

Albert Goldsmith and Doctor Andrew Webber met the next morning in the office on the eight floor of the hospital, after the results of the blood tests and x-rays and blood pressure had been analyzed by the group of doctors involved.

Dr. Webber informed Albert he had all the symptoms his Sarah had, "but, of course, not near as much as an emergency. With your permission, we will schedule you for surgery, Tuesday, at seven AM."

After signing all the papers a nurse had typed out, Alebert had quibbled, "I don't even get a copter ride."

Joyce quickly responded, "No, you had a nice van ride."

Dr. Webber informed Albert he was to enter the hospital right away in room 204.

"Take nothing but water by mouth. At twelve noon, you will be served a light lunch. There will be nothing to eat for dinner. At 6:00 PM you will be plurged and again at 9:00 PM. There will be discomfort, but very little. Oh, by the way, I understand your two daughters, Joyce and Tamala, have shown interest in the nursing profession. We have a very fine four-year college class being taught here at the hospital. With your permission, I would suggest Mrs. Clara North show them the Educational Department, " the doctor said.

Mr. Albert Goldsmith's reply was, "All the kindness and care you have shown my wife and me, we could never refuse."

Back in room 204, Albert Goldsmith was having trouble tying the strings in the gown when Tamala knocked and called.

"Dad, can I talk to you? I just wanted to thank you and Mother for letting Joyce and me start our training here. Mrs. North has been telling us that we can even work here, no more than twenty-four-hour day. We can eat here, too. There is a large medical library for students. There won't be much free-time the first year; then, after we have learned how to work efficiently, the second year there is supposed to be two-day weekends, a month of free time. The first year, students wear gray uniforms and caps, three each, and two pair special soft leather-lined, capped toe, medium low-heel and a thick cushion sole, blucher type Oxford with Velcro instead of laces. A dozen pair of thick calf-length, close-knit, white cotton hose was to be included with a pair of shoes.

"Second year students were to wear turquoise blue uniforms, the third year light cream, and the fourth year class with regulation white. All uniforms are to be "easy-care" with wrinkle-resistant collar and cuffs.

"All this program came about because a clothing and shoe manufacturer wished to prove that comfortable shoes and clothing, along with regular eight-hour shifts, would reduce fatigue by more than eighty per-cent. That company would have their own employees and doctors on duty to gather all the information and make a report every month before the hospital board and the manufacturing group.

"By the first quarter and the three reports showing improvement over the previous month, the three groups began talking win-win-win for all those participating," Tamara said.

Mr. Albert Goldsmith went through his "prep" schedule with little difficulty, saying, "These nurses explain how and why each procedure is to be done before proceeding, although the I-V needles did sting a bit," he admitted.

Joyce and Tamala brought their mother in to see how he was enjoying his "No-supper, supper," laughing as the wheeled her back to her room.

The next morning, Joyce and Tamala brought their mother in once more before Mr. Goldsmith was taken to surgery. The girls told their father that their mother would wait in her room with a nurse and "We shall go up with you and wait in the surgery-waiting room. There is a lady attendant there with a phone direct to surgery, who will let us know if a procedure is taking more time than expected and why. They did that for me and mother last week. That is another kindness the hospital provided."

Mr. and Mrs. Goldsmith sat talking with the morning of his surgery, as the nurse came in to give Albert a sedative shot, explaining, "This will make your drowsy. You did not feel the needle this time because I put it in that special tube the third shift nurse put in one her shirt. You many not feel any-more needles as I see you have two other specials just in case of emergency."

"We shall wait here five minutes then go to surgery." The nurses will wrap you tightly in a sheet, so you don't struggle and destroy all our fine work. That will last about ten seconds, after the anesthetic mask is put on."

"You and Sarah are very lucky someone knew about the symptoms of a stroke. When the brain is deprived of oxygen, the brain-cells start to deteriorate rapidly," the nurse said, referring to the quick action of Grandma Smith the week before at the Stockman's café. It had made big headlines in the Mc-Cook and Stockman papers, and she had stayed at the Stockton to look after the Goldsmith Family.

A group of nurses from surgery wheeled a gurney just as a nurse was returning Mrs. Goldsmith to her room. Embraces and a few tears were shed as Joyce and Tamala rushed to follow the group into the operating room. They were shunted to the waiting room and introduced themselves to the receptionist, who told them, "Both operating rooms are working today. Your father, Mr. Albert Goldsmith, has just entered surgery number one. This phone has a musical told. Number two surgery phone has a buzz. We want you to know so everyone won't jump every time the phone rings. We shall call you by name, then come forward and pick up your e-mail! We will answer any question at that time."

Ten minutes later, the musical phone and email machine started printing: Surgery # 1 8, 10, 97 FIRST REPORT ON ALBERT GOLDSMITH, STARTING CLOSURE PROCEDURE, PATIENT DOING WELL, BLOOD PRESSURE FANSTATIC, AFTER CUSTOMARY TWENTY MINUTE CONSTANT VITALS REPORT WILL BE READY I.C.U.

The phone from surgery number one and the printer gave the entire twenty minutes of the automatic vitals test. Each five-item test was run four times and each indicated STABLE. THE DOCTOR WILL MEET WITH YOU AT 9:00 AM in the I.C.U. waiting room. Joyce and Tamala grasped their copy of the test and rushed down the hall to the other waiting room.

Dr. A. Webber and the assisting doctor, Dr. Sam Wilson, had taken a table and pored themselves cups of coffee.

"Ask the girls if they preferred tea," said Dr. Webber. Both answered in the negative and coffee was poured.

Dr. Webber said, "Your father came through the operation just fine. We used an anesthesia that leaves the body quickly, with very little after affects. His mind is clear, there was no confusion. We clamped the artery on either side of the blockage and vacuumed the fatty-cholesterol out, made sure there were no clots released in the heart-side clamp and vacuumed a small amount of blood as it reentered the artery to prevent clots from that area. All that and closed in ninety seconds! *Team work* is the answer and practice. Every person in the room knew exactly what they were to do and when.

"Your father will remain in the intensive care unit for twenty-four hours. We have had to remind him that the three stitches are in very old material," he said with a laugh. "You two young ladies may visit one at a time for five minutes now this first visit. Have the nurse bring your mother for a first visit after lunch. I suggest you have her nurse call ICU to see if he is asleep before they go over. Oh, yes, Dr. Wilson and I have a few rounds to make this afternoon. I shall work the small child ward and Dr. Wilson has several patients in the youth ward. Choose your patients, not the doctors," Dr. Webber added.

Joyce spoke first, "I love the toddlers," she said.

"Good! Be at my office at 1:30 PM. The nurse will fix you with a smock and two note pads, just be sure to have two new pens from the PX. Tamala will go with Dr. Wilson and his nurses," Dr. Webber said.

When the two Goldsmith daughters reported to their respective doctors after lunch, they had their pens and handed their note pads and these instructions.

"On these rounds, you are expected to observe EVERYTHING IN THE ROOM, windows, doors and their location, how the ward beds are arranged. All this must be done at a glance while listening to question the patient, what bed they are assigned to. Toddlers have been known to change beds when they know they have a treatment coming they dislike. Then, tomorrow, I wish you to write a page "COMP." Don't set up all night writing; just do the best you can. In four years, you will say, "This was the easiest assignment I had in the last four years!"

When Dr. Webber entered the ward ahead of Joyce, it was not as an oversight of courtesy; it was to spare Joyce the sight of a tiny infant with a cleft lip and palate, in an incubator, with a feeding tube through a nostril into his tiny stomach.

With her first glimpse, Joyce exclaimed, "Oh may I hold him?"

Dr. Webber smiled broadly and said, "Remember the agreement to observe this round and make notes. But the real reason you need to spend to have on a special disposable cover- after scrubbing your hands clear to your eyebrows for fifteen minutes is everything must be sterilized. We will finish what we started today. Write your comp this evening. I shall have my office nurse collect all the stats that is legal. You are taking on a very heavy burden, and that is you must never discuss or disclose anything that you will hear with anyone, now or in the future."

THE NON-DISCUSSION AND NON-DISCLOSURE request from Dr. Webber startled Joyce goldsmith at first, but under the circumstances, could understand the wisdom in the request.

Dr. Webber had gone on to explain that this was what was called "an incident of birth that perhaps in two thousand births, there was a 1 percent chance of cleft incident in any nationality, sex, or color. There is no known cause. Surgery has to be done in stages of growth and age. Surgery has been very successful and the results are beautiful. A Dr. Paggett in Kansas City was a pioneer in that type of surgery, along with a team of dentist and bone specialist. During World War II, Dr. Paggett was head of plastic surgery department for all Armed services."

The author's youngest son was under Dr. Paggett's care from the time he was three days old until he was discharged from the Navy.

This was the progression that the doctor worked to fix cleft lip and nostril so the baby could be bottle-fed having extensive x-rays of the entire mouth and jaw to determine baby tooth-roots disruption and location made sure a speech teacher never let him mispronounce and ensure the tongue was relocated properly. In the progression of the author's son's growth, new things cropped up to be dealt with (Excuse the author for becoming somewhat carried away just reliving those years in those last two paragraphs, even the events from February 7,1941.).

Dr. Webber walked with his regular nurse, with Joyce trying to keep up with the fast-striding pair. Their next stop was a toddler who had scalded himself. The floor nurse and Dr. Webber quickly pulled on rubber gloves, removed the dressing to reveal a badly burned and blistered left cheek and ear. As the doctor worked, he spoke in a slightly angry tone. The child was burned by a hot coffee pout which should have never happened. The cord was a six-foot ironing cord that was looped over the edge of the counter. When Bobby went investigate, he pulled the cord when he stumbled. That is why all pots and electric-fry pans and deep fryers and equipped with cords less than three feet long, by law, the past ten years! Dr. Paggett's pilot with a team of nurses and a doctor will be here in an hour to pick up Bobby, and Jaosn will be back in his mother's arms in about ten days as explained on page twenty-two paragraph #number two.

Dr. Webber glanced at his watch. "We have just enough time to check on tiny Ella."

Joyce exclaimed, "She is hungry, she is about to swallow her thumb!"

Dr. Webber, in a sotto, voice said, "Take this young lady to our play-room tomorrow and have Clara give me a full report. It is only four weeks before her classes start, and she said she wanted some work." The doctor then continued, "Ella is undernourished. We think her mother is under some stress from over-work but still insisted Ella be breast fed. Right now, she will be bottle-fed until we find out what we can do for her mother. Ella's mother is not undergoing a series of tests. Everything the mother was doing and eating was making the baby sick. Well, I have a plane to meet. See you all tomorrow," said Dr. Webber.

Dr. Sam Wilson and his office nurse, accompanied by Tamala and her notebooks, started his rounds that afternoon by checking in with the chief youth-ward nurse at her desk. There were fifteen charts to go over. All except two were routine; these he asked a lot of questions.

"Had this boy been to physical therapy?"

"We removed a cast from his left leg Tuesday, the break is tender."

"We need a blood test, x-ray, bone density test; call an "aid" to take him to the lab now! Take a blood pressure now and call me when he returns." Then Dr. Sam Wilson thought we shall find out if anything has been overlooked.

The next patient was a boy, about twelve, suspected of having hepatitis. His tests all show hepatitis A, which is usually spread through personal contact, failure to observe personal hygiene, and sometimes, contaminated blood transfusions or dirty needles. It is very apt to destroy the liver.

"I doubt if this twelve-year-old boy has used a dirty needle, but we will have to notify the state health authorities at once; there could be an epidemic. We shall try to save this boy. Of course, the liver has some damage. We will start him on Interferon. Tamala, you m-ay watch this next step, we need a biopsy of the liver, if you feel up to it. We sedate the patient, who will feel no pain, using x-ray to guide a special long needle to the liver and collect a tiny sample from the affected area, and the lab will examine the sample."

All the above Dr. S. Wilson had ordered was performed by the emergency room while the ward-nurse arranged for an isolation room from a very frightened small youth. While the isolation room was being prepared, Dr. Wilson took his nurse and Tamala to the emergency room to watch the biopsy, then to the lab where two tiny pieces were placed between glass slides and examined. Dr. Wilson had explained every move as the three watched through a large window. Tamala, writing in short-hand, hoped she was getting it all down. Later, Dr. Wilson let Tam look in the microscope, telling her what to look for.

That evening, Tamala wrote comp in her precise hand-writing. It covered a sheet of 8 ½ by 11 unruled paper.

Joyce had written one comp that covered Bobby the baby with the cleft lip, Jacson, the burned baby, and Ella, the under-nourished baby, and the two hours in the play-room. She had to make a second draft when she realized that a lot of descriptive words could be removed and still describe her day, after she remembered Dr. Webber saying, "Always show a smiling face to the patient," which Joyce decided might be rather hard to do some-times.

Clara North, director of volunteers, spent most of the next day with Joyce and Tamala in the room of youth and toddlers. She had somehow found two sets of pink uniforms that fit and white caps were nice. Clara said, "These are absolute necessary to keep tiny fingers from pulling your hair while you are feeding them."

The two girls were next shown towels and face-clothes. They were told what to do as supply dwindled.

Joyce and Tamala had written in their notebooks every time Clara North stopped to catch her breath. When Tamala glanced down into the sad face of a three-year-old girl without-stretched arms, she turned to Clara North. Tam said, "May I pick this child up?"

"Why, yes, but I think you will find her rather damp," Clara replied and handed her a towel. "We had better go change her and find out when she has had a drink of water, too.

"Let us go over to that changing-table, I will get her chart from the front desk. I believe this child has a kidney problem. We shall see when we read her chart.

"In the meantime, let us get her changed and dry quickly. I shall have the regular duty-nurse change her. She will show you how to wash up, as we don't want to spread into the other children. Her chart will tell us that all her clothes must be kept separate in a wash-bag and washed separately, including the wash-bag."

After little Eve had been completely changed by the duty-nurse, she told Joyce and Tamala that "Eve's mother worked as head checker at the grocery on the west side of town. She was afraid she might carry the infection back to the store and contaminate the whole town. We know her, as we trade at the store, too. "Eve's mother, Mrs. Brandon, comes to our window here almost every day to see Eve and I know it just tears them both up when she has to leave. She catches a ride from the sore with a coworker, but she has to walk several blocks to catch the city bus that she rides two miles to work. She never fails to ask us to not let Eve forget her mother.

At that moment, Tamala spoke up.

"I will bring some crayons and paper. We will draw some pictures and hang them on a string across the window. That way, both will have something to look forward to each morning. Please refer to me as Eve's best friend for a while. That should not upset any-one here or at her place of work. The general public sometimes is rather insensitive. Will it be all right if I go out this evening and buy the crayons? I would like to meet and talk with her mother."

Clara North quickly said "We will meet her and Dr. Webber after we finish here. We will see how he feels about it. He might say we need crayons for all the patients in this room also."

Clara North continued showing the two prospective children-room attendants around and hoped they would remember where everything was kept. A nurse from the Physical Education Department came to give an hour of her time, devoted to strenuous exercise designed for the age-group and, or illnesses. When the time was up, the children were ready for their showers, milk and cookies, and rest period.

Those children with casts on arm, chest, foot or leg if necessity, were treated by special muscle massage and washed with soap and warm water. Joyce and Tamala showed great interest because they both knew they would be doing this in their new career. Clara North suggested they give Doctors Webber and Wilson a copy of their notes.

The first shift change an hour away, Clara North took Joyce and Tamala to the conference room of the hospital, where the two girls were exposed to the reason McCook Hospital was so well organized. Then they were on to another quick meeting with Doctors Webber and Wilson, where Clara North received her general assignments, and the two girls ran off copies of their notes.

During a lull in the conversation, Tamala could no longer contain her enthusiasm for tiny Eve. She asked the doctors their thoughts on her visiting Eve's mother and buying a box of crayons so that Eve might have some way of communicating with her mother through the window at the hospital.

"We understand the mother seems obsessed that little Eve might forget her. We wonder if the stress of the mother might be some of Eve's problem, too." In the same breath, she asked if she might stitch up a fancy trimmed little dress using washable material. "I would like to talk to her mother first as the mother might think we are usurping Eve's affection. I just want to be a friend to both of them."

Dr. Webber's reply was given quietly: "We have large department in our hospital that deals with just this type of situation. Dr. Blue has headed the Psychology Department for a number of years. He and his wife, Fay, are dining with us this evening. "I shall ask him if he has a good English language teacher free to teach Bobby his first word. Dr. Paggett says that if a child learns to pronounce words the first time they heard it correctly, they are more likely to do some thereafter.

"Now, to answer your questions, "I would suggest we move forward with some care, as I am sure that will be Dr. Blue's advice, because we could cause a disruption in the family of the little girl, which we sure want to avoid at all cost. I think, Tamala, that your plan is very good and should be given a chance.

You are very quick to size up a situation, and I hope you will continue to do so. May I suggest Clara North and you make this first visit together? Clara tires more easily, she has told me from time to time. Take advantage of the wheel chairs at the mall if she wants to shop. Just remember you are starting nurse training in about twenty days. You will need a lot of rest, too. Clara, can you think of anything we have over-looked?"

Clara's reply startled the doctor. "I think we should use those little clips with suction cups to hang those pictures on the window."

Dr. Webber replied, "You should find them and everything else you need at the mall."

Clara North turned to the girls and said, "I shall go and freshen up a bit and meet you at your mother's room. It has been so long since I have dined at Claskie's restaurant."

"That is fine with me," said Tamala, "If you promise to use the wheelchair while we shop."

"My, your car is cold!" exclaimed Clara North as she opened the door to leave for the mall."

"Oh, this isn't mine, it is my father's! He and mother gave me a small car when Joyce and I graduated from high school."

"Oh!"

"Dad sat the car out here for us to use tonight and left the air conditioner to cool it off. Mother always kept a wool blanket on her lap. I will shut it off for a while."

When they arrived at the mall, Tamala parked near the motorized chairs and espied one with two seats and a large basket. She brought it out to the car and seated Clara North. She drove to an alcove near the entrance of Claskie's restaurant, parked the chair, and entered the dining room. Dressed conservatively, the two ladies were a picture of youth and the beautiful silver hair age. Youth was to discover that spike heels were not made for shopping in.

Mr. Claskie and wife, Dora, were at the reservation's counter as the ladies walked in. Dora said, "We have been watching for you. Dr. Webber called and wanted us to remind you about your heart medicine. We have a nice table close to the dance floor." Turning to Tamala, she said, "It is the table where she and husband Don sat every Saturday evening. Clara just loved the slow waltz. One night, they were chosen King and Queen of the Ball."

Tamala saw a scring [nbbande4] remembrance cross the face of Clara, and broke into the conversation.

"We promised to get our shopping done before the evening rush. We had better eat a bite."

"Oh, I do tend to rattle on!" said Mrs. Claskie as she showed them to their table and summoned the waitress, who came with spotless crystal glasses of water and the menus.

Clara North glanced at it and asked for the large print. *Oh!* thought Tamala, *Clara's eyes are falling!* and then she looked at her own menu- and it was printed in Italian! Clara is so considerate of every one's feelings; their menus were now printed in English.

They ordered a small lean steak with mushroom gravy, decaffeinated coffee, a small dessert and white bread. They asked if it could be brought quickly, as they wished to do some shopping this evening.

Their dinner almost over, a young man with very blond hair walked over to their table.

"Aunt Clara, I tried to call you early this evening. Are you feeling well this evening? My mother is over behind a column worrying you might be ill."

Pressing a call button, she turned to Tamala and said, "This my youngest grandson, Howard North. He starts to law school this fall."

Mr. Claskie was standing beside Clara, who asked to have chairs brought for Mr. North and his mother, who wished to join us. They will use the table and the rest of the evening. I presume they have already ordered.

Before all were seated, Clara North introduced Tamala and Mrs. Evelan North with some brevity, saying, "Tam, this is my oldest sister, Evelan."

Two waitresses who laid the table for the two turned to leave, Clara spoke sharply, "Please, Bring Tam and me another pot of tea. We have just enough time before our parking runs out on wheelchair."

Tamala glanced sharply at Clara, who never changed expression, then at Evelan, who had a slight smirk on her lips. Tamala thought, *Oh, the air about this table is getting frosty.*

The two drank their tea in silence as the music started drifting from the pit. Howard asked Aunt Clara if she felt well enough for a turn around the floor.

"Not this evening, it is almost for an appointment we must keep. I know your mother is a very good dancer."

Tamala quickly helped Clara into the chair and asked Clara if they had better go right to the head-checker, Mrs. Brandon. Clara said, "Yes, it is better to be ten minutes early than one minute late, if you are going to catch the bus.

But if we are going to use the crayons as an excuse for a chance meeting we better go to the stationary department quickly."

Tamala and Clara found a packet of the brightest colors, another packet that were less brilliant, a package of white typing pad, another with all colors of the rainbow, and a small packet of digestible. With these articles, they proceeded to another counter and found a suitable briefcase.

By this time, Tamala's spike-heels were bothering her. She said, "Let us find the check-out!"

The position of Mrs. Brandon was to help all the checkers whenever they made an error, punched the wrong key, if the machine jammed, or even what to do when the machine printed the wrong prices because of a price change that was never entered on the memory-tape. All-in-all, it was a very stressful position, with many of the customers becoming angry.

The store had a policy that each person was to spend on the old-rattler (old practice machine) at least three eight hour days, but still, there were glitches. The men who were actually assigned to the mechanical repair work, having gone to the factory school for up to a year, sometimes had glitches, too, though these were more easily accounted for.

Clara North and Tamala checked out at the first check-stand that was clear of customers. When they finished, they inquired where they might find Mrs. Brandon. They were told she was on a fifteen-minute break, possibly in the lunchroom for a bit of tea.

Clara and Tamala drove the wheelchair to the lunchroom, which was located between the snack bar and the deli meats and cheese, either by chance or just good merchandising.

Mrs. Brandon was seated at a table with a checkered tablecloth. She had just finished her sandwich and hot tea when Clara North walked over Tamala parked the wheelchair. Clara North introduced Tamala Goldsmith as a young lady who planned to start nurse training the day after Labor Day, to work some after school, but claimed she had no real skills except housework and drawing pictures for her own entertainment.

Clara said, "I have heard you tell her, on several occasions, not to ever forget you. We know you won't ever, and so does little Eve, but she just can't express herself. We think Eve might be weeping in frustration. Let us say Eve draws a picture of you holding her in your arms, and you pretend you really are. Maybe we can get through to that beautiful little girl. I'll bet no one has checked her eye-sight lately. I don't remember reading anything about the eye-sight lately. I don't remember reading anything about the eyes in her charts."

Mrs. Elva Brandon's reply started Clara and Tamala.

"Well, as you know, I work nights and my husband works six days a week at the limestone quarry hauling stone to the crusher. He has Sunday off and I have Monday off. He never helps around the house. I wish he would do his own laundry, that limestone dust just covers his cloths and makes great big sores on his back where the truck rubbed. He does wear a mask, otherwise his lungs would be solid concrete."

All valid reasons, no doubt, but she avoided my question completely, thought Clara, *I shall let Tamala talk to her while I drink my tea.*

Tamala poured Elva Brandon another cup of tea and asked her how long Eve had been in the hospital.

"Too long," was the reply. " A week ago she had a fever and I took her to the emergency. They drew blood for tests and called Doctor Weber. I heard him say every test so far has been so uncertain we should put her in isolation-room and make tests every hour and giver her something to reduce the fever. The nurses will know how to draw blood without it being so painful. Dr. Web-ber explained the reason the tests take so long is that we don't know how long it should be incubated and how active it will be after incubation."

At this point, Elva began to weep and Tamala instinctively reached across the table to hold her hands in reassurance. She felt a rough wart-like growth about the size of a nickel near the web of Elva's left thumb was starting to bleed. Quickly, Tamala drew a new handkerchief and covered the area, saying, "This will keep it off your clothes. How long have you had this growth?"

"Oh, I just noticed it this morning. It was only about the size of a large head of a pin this morning and I thought nothing about it," replied Elva.

"Clara North, will you call the store nurse? This should have a bandage on it, and if the nurse and store-manager can see it now, there should be no problem about insurance," said Tamala.

By the time the manager arrived, Clara North had contacted Dr. Webber, who felt Mrs. Brandon should come to the emergency-room at the hospital, "at least until we find out more about this. Please ask the store-nurse not to apply any kind of dye to the area," said Dr. Webber.

She dressed the hand and said, "That looks like a blood-wart to me. It should be removed. I just got off the phone with Dr. Webber. He said we should not let any blood touch the skin, as that is the way they are apt to spread. The store-nurse said that Dr. Webber had an ambulance on its way, and should be here any minute…"

Clara North quickly gave the ambulance crew the drill on the situation. Mrs. Elva Brandon was on her way to the emergency-room.

Tamala and Clara proceed to the parking lot with their purchases and loaded them into the car. Just then, Tamala exclaimed, "Should we pick up a pair of soft house-slippers for Mrs. Brandon? She will be there without a thing."

"All right, I will buy some under things," replied Clara.

By the time they got to the hospital, Tamala added a tiny pair of felt slipper-boots and two tiny dolls. "For when we have to tell Eve her mother is in the hospital, too," explained Tamala.

By the time Clara and Tamala entered the hospital emergency room, Mrs. Elva Brandon had been x-rayed and biopsied. Blood samples had also been drawn and sent to the lab. Elva was resting comfortably in isolation ward at-room 620. She had talked to her husband on the phone while at the emergency room, and he had come still dressed in his rock-dust-covered work clothes. The ER Doctor asked if he might collect a large sample. He said, "Sure, my pockets feel like they are full of ground rock. You should see my back. It rubs on the back of the truck. It is a sold mass of sores."

The ER doctor asked Mr. Brandon to give samples and a biopsy sure would help settle a theory that there was a pre-historic virus in rock-dust!

"We just might be able to find the answer to your daughter's problem also. She is too precious a child to be in isolation."

Mr. Brandon, when told the rock dust might be a suspect in the illness of his daughter, was somewhat concerned about the project of the rock-quarry being closed down because of the rock-dust, as the city had been complaining it settled on the roof of homes and windows, where even a heavy dew sets up like cement.

With the whole Brandon family in the hospital waiting for their various tests, which will take more than a week to complete, Tamala spent some time with her mother and father, and of course, with Clara North and the tiny elf, Eve. Tamala cut some interesting pictures from a magazine and helped Eve glue them to the sheets of colored paper. Tamara would then wrote little notes and have Eve trace along the lines and sign them Eve, who was so proud when she got it correct and showed them to all the nurses. She promised to save them for her mother when she got well.

The time for the Goldsmith daughters by now had narrowed to two weeks to start their nurse training. Their parents, on the other hand, had been discharged from the hospital.

Joyce got on the phone to Paradise Village and spoke to John Smith and Erma. She asked if their harvest was over down there. She was told that it was and they were just about to call her and see if everyone was ready to come back to Kansas. When told the Goldsmiths were both discharged from the hospital, John smith said, "Erma and I shall bring Chet Curtis to drive your father's car so he can ride in the van in comfort. We can be there about two PM tomorrow. We shall stay at a hotel and rest and go to the mall that evening. We hear there is a nice Club there."

John Smith and Erma had been calling his father's gift van The Luxury Liner since they had returned from McCook hospital. His father had the village sign painter paint it on both sides. He reminded John he had better store the van in his agency garage or the water in the rest-room tanks would freeze this winter.

Chet Curtis, the college student who hauled wheat and wanted to learn the co-operative structure so he would be able to help John Smith and Erma start his Elderly Car community, would drive the Liner for us this trip because he had all the licenses to drive the big trucks, which really all the liner is.

John's father, Jim, planned to go with us this trip. He was also interested in getting the healthcare center started and completed.

The Liner left the next morning after the passengers and driver had a breakfast of ham, eggs, hot cakes, and coffee prepared by the two hard-working farm-girls who had stayed on after harvest to help with the house-work for the elderly couple, Pa (Jake) Smith and Ma (Eva).

Jim Smith had asked his son, John, if he might bring along three of his best salesmen and their wives. They had been spreading the news about what John proposed in a hush manner. They knew everyone in the country, having gathered a lot of information on the number of elderly in the county and their thoughts on a proper retirement. I think you will be surprised by the number of things that need to be done first.

The luxury liner Chet Curtis drove left the Jake (Pa) Smith farm-stead at 6:00 AM August 6, 1999, and arrived at the Stockman's Café two hours later. After a hearty breakfast of hotcakes, eggs, bacon, and a glass of orange juice, they were on their way to McCook, Nebraska.

They arrived at the McCook Hospital where they were greeted by Mr. and Mrs. Goldsmith and their two daughters, Joyce and Tamala, who had just come in from a walk around the hospital grounds.

Mr. Albert Goldsmith informed them that the hospital administration had made a commitment to meet with them all in the hospital conference that evening at seven PM.

"It had some equipment that will be used. The room is sound-proofed. We just might be in town several days!"

"We should make reservations for our room at the hotel, eat lunch, and get some rest from your journey. [nbbande5]"

All had been assigned their rooms on the eighth floor, because John Smith said he wanted to say he had lived high this trip! All the rooms face the main street and a museum building almost as high as the hotel. The group descended to the dining room for lunch. At lunch, several of the McCook city dignitaries were introduced by the manager of the hotel. Jim Smith and his son, John, were the primary boosters at this impromptu conversation, saying they were interested in the care of the elderly and how they were being cared for after they became unable to care for themselves.

"We have heard so many stories of poor care, neglect, unsanitary conditions of rooms, improper diet, and loss of appetite from ill-fitting dentures-that sometimes get misplaced and no even noticed. We have heard that your hospital and care homes here and in McCook have the best rating in the states." At this point, John Smith took over the conversation.

"We are, in our village in fact, our entire county is a farming community. We all have pride in our avocation; unfortunately, many of us are my father's age or older.

"My father, Jim Smith, was injured in a farm accident while helping his father, my grandfather. It was my father's intention in his youth to become a medical doctor. But after the accident, his crippled left hand stopped his dream of being a surgeon, while knowing he had to provide for his elderly father and mother. Fortunately, he had a talent for selling autos and trucks and now owns the agency. I was raised to believe that it was I who was to fulfill his dream.

"I have now made arrangement with my grandparents whereby they will continue to live on their farm. We have arranged for competent help in the household and the cattle and the field work. These employees are under their supervision.

"This fall I shall start medical school and my fiancée shall start nurses training. We feel that it is in our future to have competent care for the elderly in our country. We are asking suggestions and council. It is our intent to first start a community center for the elderly, where they can enjoy many activities, as well as proper exercise and diet.

"We have a good medical doctor in our community, but he is now almost sixty-five years old. Additionally, his workload is much heavier now than a year ago."

John called a halt to his talk as he noticed the wives were becoming restless by saying, "We are all tired from our journey, we should retire to our rooms and rest and hour or so and be fresh for our meeting with members of the hospital board. This lunch is adjourned."

All members of the group made mental notes of what they wished to discuss at the meeting this evening, as they rested in the security of their rooms.

The group from the mythical Paradise Village, Kansas, had been well coached by John Smith and his fiancée, Erma, before they were to depart for the conference with the hospital administration.

John Smith and Erma had prepared a folio listing the things the citizens of Paradise Village might need and perhaps should be made available to them to provide healthcare that preserves their dignity. Many of these people are their friends and neighbors.

The group went down to the hotel dining-room and made a short ride to the north side of town, in the Luxury Liner driven by Chet Chester Curtis, who was warned that he was to have them all back to the hospital no later than six fifteen PM. Also, Joyce and Tamala wanted to show them little Bobby and little Eve, if they were still awake even if little Eve could only be seen through a window.

The ride about the town was nice but uneventful, going through long, wide, tree-lined streets, with beautiful homes freshly painted, most with large curved glass bay-windows and set well back from the street. Many had wide circular drives, with about as many square feet of ground to either side and to the rear, which allowed for four-car garages on the first floor and small apartments for living quarters for the chauffeurs. Another building housed the working tools of the master gardener and the storage of supplies. When the driver turned to return to the hospital, someone in the group remarked, "I think the homes are beautiful. I hope they are happy and content. I wonder if they ever think of the hardships to the generations that settled this city?" They all agreed they would rather live in their own Paradise Village.

On the way back from the hospital, Joyce thought of the vow Dr. Webber had reminded her when they first talked about her entering nurse training: "By word or deed, I will not do harm to those in my care." She stood on the aisle of the van, gripping the back of two seats until her fingers were turning white. She began to speak, at first in a quavering voice that son become strong and vibrant as she spoke.

"I hope, in my life-time I never forget that vow. We may not get to see little Bobby this evening because I did not ask Dr. Webber's permission first.

"I shall recount you a story just as Dr. Webber told me to that morning.

"One morning while I was a first year medical student, a group of us were discussing birth defects and what proper attitude a doctor should have to remain true to his God when he feels sure a patient has beyond any possible chance of living a pleasant and happy useful life.

"The old professor looked at us with his sad old eyes and said, 'compassion, compassion, compassion must rule your life.'" He told us this story: 'When I was a young doctor in the hills of Kentucky, my first birthday was for a young couple living on a hard scrabble hillside farm in a log-cabin. The first time I saw Sarah James come to my office riding an old plough mule and carrying a basket of chicory root she had been gathering, complaining that she had been living on sassafras tea and laudanum syrup most of the time and it just makes her sicker, I lost it all. I explained to her that it was the syrup that was making other her and the baby so sick. My wife and I could see that she was about to deliver. We put her in our bedroom and I carried in two tubs of water and went to a neighbor to have him locate Sarah James's husband. By the time I returned, another neighboring couple had stopped and helped my wife bathe, soothe, and comfort her as best they could, considering the fact that we had just moved in two days before."

Joyce Goldsmith continued on the vivid image of the suffering Sarah, repeating word for word the story that Dr. Webber had told her and her sister, Tamla.

"I had no inkling of the background history of this young couple. I looked through all my medicines and powders to find something that would relieve Sarah of her pain and not harm her baby. I never felt so inadequate in my life. This gentle neighbor lady turned to me and said, "Well, if we are going to turn this baby, we better get started." I had given her some liquid to help endure the pain, I hoped. And with our bare but well scrubbed hands, we delivered a crippled live human being. As she lay ther ein the bed, all manner of thoughts raced through my mind. As I tied the cord and severed her from her mother forever, I thought she was a beautiful baby. But how will she survive in this hard world with a withered left leg, and live a happy life? I thought, *I can just turn my back and in a few minutes and she will be gone and that will relieve everyone of responsibilities.* Then I realized the mothers in that room had been praying for hours. Then I thought as if the lord had laid his hand on my shoulder and I thought of the word "compassion" and the vow that we made when we graduated from medical school.'

"'But this story has a beautiful ending,' the elderly medical professor said with a chuckle as he noticed the tense expressions of those in his class that day.'

"'The mother, Sarah, did survive under the care of my wife and the midwife, Beca, and myself, although she might never bear another child. Sarah stayed at our place for six weeks. In those days, ten days in bed was a must for a first birth. You see, our knowledge was not great in those days in early America. We learned a lot about the James family that summer, just from the people who came just to see Sarah and her new baby.'

"'These Gentle ladies never spoke of little Sarena's deformity. They came bringing gifts of clothing and some found tatting made with the tiniest shuttle and their husbands came with fresh butchered beef, and another never missed a day to bring a pail of fresh milk for that beautiful little baby. Then miracles began to happen, or so it seems. My wife, feeling somewhat tired from doing unaccustomed duties, played a happy melody, hoping to raise her spirit and frame of mind, when Sarah James started singing to little Sarah Brenda James. When questioned, Sarah related she had played all through high school and college where her parents still lived. "You are welcome to play any time you are here," said my wife. "Would you like to play now? I will hold the baby," who had begun to squirm around. At the first note, the baby lay quiet and as her mother played on, that tiny withered leg began to move, as though keeping time to the music! I could hardly wait to tell my husband, the doctor (of course, I did not say a word to Sarah- I didn't want to raise her hope too high- although we found out much, much later the reason Sarah had quit playing singing and playing was Sarahbrenda [nbbande6] kicked so hard, it was uncomfortable.'

"I started to write to the Doctors Medical Journal to share my notes on baby Sarabrenda and ask if anyone was making a study on withered appendages. Soon, my office was flooded with letters from all over the nation offering all kinds of assistance. As the child grew older, she also began to play the piano and her notoriety spread and she was offered scholarships in fine schools of music."

Joyce Goldsmith continued on with the narrative of the elderly medical professor's story to his class.

"I had my practice in Lost Dog Hollow for ten long years. We had a nine year-old daughter and an eight-year-old son by that time when a letter came from Boston, offering me the position as teacher in the medical department.'

"That letter from Boston really changed our lives, or perhaps I should say, our way of living. My wife had to change from a drudge to a beautiful other to our children almost overnight, it seemed. This new life we were to live seemed a miracle. There was a small library where the children could bring books home, read, and return properly. There was a small library where the children could bring books home, read, and return properly. My wife no longer had to make do for clothing for any of the family. In Lost Dog Hollow, we had all worn our patches with pride. We had become one of the villagers of Lost Dog and never realized it, until our first snub in Boston, But snubs are best to be forgotten and forgiven.'

"'My wife and I were to enjoy another button-popping miracle and that didn't happen until twenty years later.'

"'My wife and I received an invitation to a recital at the Great Hall where we were to be the honored quests.'

"'As we walked into the hall, we were ushered to seats in the front row, where we sat listening to Sarabrenda James play the most interesting music for over an hour. There I sat, tears streaming as I thought of the hour of her birth and the unseen hand on my shoulder, my vow, my room of praying ladies, and of compassion.'"

The Luxury Liner was now drawing near the hospital, and the spellbound passengers' faces' expressions were as though they had lived the life of the sad-eyed elderly medical professor as they filed off, as Mr. C. Curtis played a few notes of "Come Walk with Him," on the musical air horn as a salute. He then handed his recorder and tape to Joyce's father and asked him to play it at their meeting tonight. He added, "Ask how many want copies and I shall have them made, no cost."

Clara North and Dr. Webber had just finished checking the pile of papers stacked neatly in trays to the right of each chair at the long conference table. On the left lay the folio from the Paradise Village group. In front of each chair were a microphone and a play-back machine in case someone was asked to re-peat what had been said.

Dr. Webber rose from his chair at the head of the table, flanked by Dr. Wilson and his secretary.

Dr. Webber's words floated from the microphone.

"Oh, God, our heavenly Father, hear our plea: Guide us in our plans for the betterment of all mankind. Should we ever disagree, correct us. Let no man put asunder our feeble accomplishments. We ask in thy Son's name, Amen.

"To start this meeting off, I have been asked to play a tape that was made just an hour ago by the daughter of Mr. Albert and Sarah Goldsmith."

The voice of Joyce Goldsmith, quavering at first, then growing strong and vibrant, floated from each speaker. The audience sat spellbound until Dr. Webber, in a strained voice, said, "There are Kleenex tissues in each drawer in front of each chair." The sound of drawers being opened could be heard. The tape continued, until the musical air-horn rendered the salute.

Dr. Webber's voice once more floated from the speakers.

"Those of you who wish to receive a copy of Miss Goldsmith's tape, at no cost, please leave your name and address with Mrs. Clara North and it will be mailed to you. Once again, I call this meeting to order. Mr. John Smith and his fiancée, Erma, are planning to further their education in this field this fall. Frankly, we are here at the hospital are trying to convince them they can receive the same training here. If we are unsuccessful, we will wish them success in their new schools."

Turning to John Smith, Dr. Webber smiled and said, "John, we here at McCook Hospital have spent an entire year with a group of trained individual, doctors, nurses, nurse aids, supervisors, safety personnel, all working in their own fields in the commercial industries and observing health and work habits that can increase production and eliminate many incidences of injury. This group find many things that are similar to ours here at the hospital, such as fatigue and stress. We here have enormous amount of that! We reduced the number of hours of all registered nurses (RN) at no reduction of pay. Of course, we had to create another shift of nurses and supervisors for the fourth shift and that called for more trained personnel, which was not a problem as we had a class graduate about the time we needed them. There were many changes to follow, such as the required white cool weave caps and pant suit uniforms with large pockets and a clip for their three-inch nurse special sheers. The fact that the uniforms were of pre-starched material that required no pressing was another perk for the nurses.

"The group that supervised our training had started with our supervisory personnel, working in small groups. They used a special manual that had animated diagram showing how a certain tone of voice could be misinterpreted as slanderous remark and cause a negative attitude. Remember, words once spoken are hard to retrieve."

"It is not a normal attitude to dislike one's duties and obligations one has been trained for. Listen to your people, drink a cup of tea with them, and find out what is wrong. Some people brighten up sometimes just from a word of praise of their work. Others prefer to avoid the limelight. Just remember that in our profession, we are obligated to follow Time-Proven Safe Procedures."

Doctor Webber concluded his presentation and turned the meeting over to John Smith, who said, "There is great wisdom in every word of your presentation. I hope everyone in my group has it on their tape, because at present, we do not even have a building. It is our desire to learn if our plan to build a community gathering place where the elderly can get together, have birthday parties, playcards, have supervised exercise classes, and classes on health is feasible. We think this approach should keep them in their own homes a bit longer until supervised assisted living apartments could be built.

"We know not what companies make furniture and bedding, among other things, appropriate for this type of living that Erma, my fiancée, describes as a honeymoon many of them never had time for those hard years."

About 7:30 PM, a member of the group doing the study on affiance for the McCook Hospital spoke up.

"My company is located in Omaha. Just tell us how much ground we would have, how many stories high, and the material to be used in the buildings. We know most of Kansas building standard codes and will consult with Topeka building codes office before ordering any material."

"This is exactly the information we are looking for! Can you assemble a group that will set up a system to keep track of the overall construction with about 99.99 percent accuracy? Materials come in and need to be checked that something else has not be substituted. That takes a master lead journey-man for every trade!

"Then there is labor contract requirements that need strict compliance. We in Paradise Village would be aghast should there be a labor strike!

"If you are really interested, my father is the head of the company and my brother is second in command. They are at Holbrook tonight with our demonstration van. May I call him?" John Smith glanced at Erma and said, "Please do."

Ray Albertson and his eldest son, Joe, were eating breakfast at the hotel café when John and Erma came for their first cup of coffee. The hotel manager made the introductions. John Smith remarked that Mr. Albertson was real prompt in keeping appointments.

Ray said, "Oh, we had the van all packed ready to return to Omaha headquarters when my youngest son called all excited about some speech someone had made that evening. We were only fifty miles from here, and we hadn't seen Rod and his family since the Fourth of July out in Denver. I have some personnel setting up some equipment. They should be done by the time your group has finished breakfast.

"In the mean-time, let us talk about your plans for a community center and its location, the retirement and assisted living apartments themselves, and the light, water, and heating. How about air conditioning wide Plexiglas-covered walkways through formal gardens? How about tall, hard maple trees, security lightning all over the grounds and covered walkways, health and security stations? One should place duct line phone, TV, security, emergency call each room, fire alarms, fire extinguishers, proper locations by code, and above all else, proper emergency exit signs that are backlight-equipped sensors; every long hallway would have chargeable battery floodlights that light the halls in case of power failure, or filled with some of these; we also need sensors that report their condition to the central dispatch-room that should know where each maintenance man and his apprentice is working. To assure compliance, all apparatuses are being tested for proper operation. This alone should eliminate most arraignment with city and federal inspectors. And any time we can stay in compliance with all, we are apt to increase our number of elderly residents." Ray Albertson added, "It will also decrease the insurance but not eliminate them. We have just covered a very small part of the construction!"

"Mr. Ray Albertson, we need to know about the size of each room in the apartments and something about the layout of the land. Should there be a large storage basement, or will there be apartments in the basement? Is the land free of legal encumbrances?"

"I can have a survey crew and check the outer boundaries, as there is bound to be some state and county roads involved on a section of land. We should know and have these kind of situations settled well before any construction starts. I'll be you did not realize employees in the building trades really take pride in their work. Many point with pride at buildings, saying, 'We were there during dedication ceremonies.' That is the kind of men that I enjoy having on the job.

"Let us all go out to the demonstration van and look at some of the work we have done around the country.

"Do you realize your group already has some management skills? You could form a corporation and finance it by selling shares. Just an idea! We will talk to the older men in your group. I think after we run our films, they will have a good concept of the necessity of a long-term investment plan."

John's reply was a question: "What do you think of a co-operative arrangement similar to our grain elevators? About everyone in our county that farms and raises wheat, oats, soy-beans for human food consumption is into it. Some co-ops even operate a drying plant for alfalfa and process it into live-stock feed. They know how they are funded by two $25.00 membership shares that would pay a small percentage of interest on the amount over actual operating expense. This membership would also pay small percentage from the profit, after all operating expenses and reasonable amount set aside for inflation and unexpected expense. This amount is not to exceed thirty five percent as directed by the board of trustees, consisting of nine members elected from the membership at the board meeting held on the first Monday in March at the regular annual meeting. All interest are to be held in escrow and each member advised in a statement mailed to them showing the exact amount of each category and the percentile used and the total amount held in escrow that would be ready to be used at each retirement when they entered their apartment. Of course, the cost of membership would have to start at $100.00 each; that could be raised or lowered by a majority vote of the membership requesting the board to make the change. It's a sort of pre-retirement insurance that should ensure each member an equal and adequate care in their late elderly retirement, without too much dissension among the membership."

Ray Albertson's reply was typical, based on his many years of experience: "Your idea of co-op financing is a concept I had never thought of for healthcare. It has some flaws, but they can be corrected by proper wording in the contract and the bylaws of the membership. At this time, let me show some of the work my company has done in the healthcare industry. I think can consolidate any of my plans to please everyone."

The two groups then moved from the hotel dining room to the parking lot, still babbling with enthusiasm about John Smith's co-op system to raise funds for retirement, not realizing that it would require a certain amount of frugality on the part of each member of the corporation for a generation of waste not want not?

The two groups moved into the Traveling Demonstration Showroom. They settled into comfortable chairs and began watching the film of the deteriorating building in a poor neighborhood followed by a film showing the same neighborhood after it had been replaced by a new six-story retirement home, followed by a film showing the inside before it was finished after a year of occupation.

Both groups were shown film of apartment buildings with extra large apartments with combined living and dining room and two bedrooms somewhat smaller. The kitchen was funny equipped and arranged with easy access to the dining area. The two bedrooms were either to the right or left of the living room, with large walk-in clothes closets. The rooms were somewhat smaller than the living room, allowing more space in the bath-room for an under-cover washer-dryer. All of the larger apartments would be located to the sixth floor for occupancy by the younger retirees who wanted a home to return to after extensive trips to the old country.

The group from Paradise Village was shown several room designs, but they could not make any conclusive decision. It was the wives of the car-salesman they should make another survey of the country, because they knew that some of the farm women had beautiful china cabinets that they would willingly part with, as well as other heirlooms.

Ray Albertson, the building contractor, was free and clear of any legal encumbrance since the section of land they wished to build on was being donated by the grandparents of John Smith-who owned it- to the new co-op company. Ray said, "If Jake Smith really does not need the section of land to make a living we should accept it. We can build on the other half and expand later.

"These salesman and their wives can get their survey started. I will call Omaha and have them have my survey team down in Paradise Village. I shall have my office make a model. If we can fill one hundred apartments in the first six weeks after we finished, the co-op should be in the win-win position."

The wives of the salesmen of Jim Smith auto agency began a list of incentives they could use for their sales talk to the farm wives. Will there be a chapel near? Will there be several denominations, and if so, would each have a designated store-level? We already know that in harvest time, everyone is in the fields until the crops are in and stored. But any other time, most are very devout in their attendance.

Could the present co-op community grocery be enticed to move to our location on a huge parking lot, so that our elderly might shop via Plexiglas-covered driveway with their electric chairs, with an assistant until their health made it no longer advisable?

But what we wish to stress most would be the fact that there would be so much less house-work and no outside chores to do. Those farm-ladies have long-earned their right to a tranquil retirement.

"This is Ray Albertson speaking now: I am convinced that you ladies should become floor-managers. I have heard more ideas in the last twenty minutes than in some group meetings. Keep your ideals high and you will see this thing through. I think you just might have early retirement in mind, too," Ray said with a laugh. "Don't wait too long!"

Eva (Ma) and Jake (Pa) Smith and Albert and Sarah Goldsmith, who had been talking with their children, raised their hands in unison. Ray laughed and said, "I don't have room up here for all of you, so I shall ask Albert and Jake to come forward and represent the others."

Jake and Albert walked to the front of the room, and Jake said, "We wish to be the first two families to move into the suite's top floor east end," adding as an aside, "Albert has promised not to move in any of his range bulls if he can stable four range ponies out at his farm!

"Just isn't enough housing here or the surrounding village to take care of all the labor force. We are thankful this is the county seat, so a lot of land records are required should we have a need to close any county or township roads." Little did he know that the closing of the county and township roads was entirely different from how it was done in Nebraska.

Ray Albertson was about to close the meeting when he turned to John Smith and said, "It is my hope-and about everyone I had talked to at McCook hospital, especially Dr. Webber and Clara North that you would have at least part of your medical training right here in McCook. I understand that another meeting with them today could be very advantageous for you and your friend, Erma, in your professional careers. I don't know just what they have in mind, but be assured they are far too busy to get concerned too long about your careers. I understand you will be twenty-one tomorrow. We should celebrate it, because one never has a second twenty-first birthday. Just use good judgment."

John Smith and his loyal friend, Erma, did make an appointment that very morning, after it had become clear to him that his that his problem was he had been unable to make a decision, mostly because of being too anxious about being wrong even after having made an elaborate study of the situation. Dr. Webber told him that because of his age, he had not done many things that required that kind of logic. By the time you have four years of college and about six years of medical practice, you will wonder why it ever bothered you; you will know why it did.

"You will experience another type of logic that I will hope will prevent you from making very serious mistakes. Just remember, confidence in your ability and belief in the Lord will see you through."

Turning to Joe Albertson, Ray said, "You are my eldest son. I think you had better run this show for a short time. I just remembered I told your mother sixty years ago that we would return to the place we were married. It was quite primitive at the time, but your mother fell in love with region around the Royal Gorge. I had been working in my first construction after I had finished college, when I met the most beautiful lady in the world. She called me last evening and asked me if I had remembered the vow we made sixty years ago. She said she had talked to my pilot last evening; he said the plane is ready for services and for you to meet us McCook air-port at 11:00 A.M. We will have lunch in Denver. Could we just rent a car there then you and I drive the same route we did on our way back to Nebraska place? The territory is so beautiful."

On the flight to Denver, Evelan disclosed some more plans. For one thing, the pilot's wife, a very good friend, had disclosed her desire to visit Colorado Springs and the surrounding countryside.

"Can't we park the big plane at the hangar in Denver? We will take them to the springs through rent-a-car while we go on the Gorge. Oh, I have looked forward to this trip for so long. I think we will enjoy it even more than our trip to the Island or the trip to England, because you were always in such a hurry to get back to the company."

Ray Albertson turned to his wife and said, "What would you say if I retired before I had a traditional heart attack? I am about to start building a bealth center that will be the best equipped and managed in all the USA?"

She replied in a soft voice, "Soon, I hope. I have been so lonely these past years."

It was then he told her about the group in Paradise Village and their dreams.

Arriving in the Denver, the pilot began talking to the control tower in the standard gibberish, and somewhere in the interchange, the pilot turned to Mr. Albertson and said, "Your coach is waiting. We are to land on runway 2 and continue on to hangar 2 where it is waiting. You and the ladies look it over while I stabilize this mule in hangar 2 and sign in. I'll tell them we will be gone about eight days. I have another ferry the next day to New England. I hope my wife will have some free time, as that is also the time I ask for the yearly plane cheek-up."

Meanwhile, out on the hangar apron, Ray discovered, as he was in the process of loading the baggage into the limousine, that the ladies had packed a huge picnic basket that they planned to open as soon as they found a good place on the way down to the Springs. All Ray could say was, "There may be big bad bears out there."

The pilot, Avery Graham, had been ferrying for various corporations ever since he had been discharged from the US Air Force. It paid well and above all, the corporations keep their planes in the best condition. After all, who would want to be the company manager and sales force flying in an obsolete plane?

Of late, Annabell had gone on several trips and while she seemed to enjoy the trips, she kept saying, "We never had a real honeymoon because of the war. Let this trip be the best ever. The mountains are so beautiful this time of year. Maybe you should retire also. With Jim away in college, it sure is lonely."

Avery replied, "Maybe we should start making plans. I would like a room full of the best wood-working tools and time enough to use them," he added.

Annabell suggested, "Maybe we should work in some church community work, too?"

When the limousine left Denver, Avery Graham said, "This instrument panel may confuse me a little, but where are the wings?"

Annabell, always quick with a quip, said, "If you should go over a cliff, you will wish you had a parachute also. Didn't you read the instructions before starting assembling?"

This bit of horse-play lasted long enough to be well out of the city, and on a course set for the Springs, when Evelan Albertson called, "Start looking for a nice shady spot to eat! My Omaha breakfast isn't going to last much longer. Ray, you have almost a hundred miles to drive to the Royal Gorge.

"Oh, it has been sixty years, but I can still visualize that beautiful sunset as we sat on that porch of that little log cabin after our marriage in that little church in the canyon. It was as if the whole world was opening its arms to us, don't you remember, Ray? Everyone was so kind to us that day. And years later, after Tim was born, I just couldn't wait for him to grow enough to understand the glory of that sunset. That year Tim had scarlet fever, he was fifteen, and you were working on some western hotel in some western city and I had to call you home. You had driven straight through, and you looked it, too. Then, the doctor quarantined the home and you couldn't return to work. I remember after you talked to Tim he seemed to brighten up then you lay down on the cot in the garage. You never moved for six hours and started to laundry all the bed clothes and everything in sight.

"While the dryer was running, you came in with some cold towels you had put in the freezer, saying you had washed them in a strong disinfectant, just like I am doing with the laundry. We sure hoped it would help. When is the doctor coming in? I want to know if there is anything I am doing correctly. We need more disinfectant and is there a better brand? Breakfast is on the table; eat then get some sleep. I will call you when the doctor arrives."

Evelan Albertson continued her lament that Tim had never had the thrill of watching a Colorado sunset when Annabell Graham glanced at her husband, who was using his cell phone while driving the limousine.

"If you are to drive and use that thing, we better stop and have our picnic in Castle Rock now!" she said in a sharp tone. "We are on Highway 83. Those hills to our right are not the mountains. And we are getting hungry." she added with emphasis.

In a few minutes, they were parked in a shady picnic area not much different from those along the highways of Kansas and Nebraska. There was no litter, restroom was clean, and clean drinking fountain was near their table. This wasn't just quite like the picture the ladies had in mind when they made their plans in Omaha. However, it would accomplish what the devious Annabell had in mind.

After all had enjoyed the lunch and were gathering things, Annabell said, "I bought a special notebook just to record all the joyous things we do or see on this trip. Avery, will you please help me retrieve it from my luggage?"

Walking to the limousine, Annabell handed Avery a note that had the address and phone number of the place where Tim Albertson was staying at the school. "If the housemother answered, if someone else answered, talk to her so Tim would not think there had been an accident. Make sure she won't get the message mixed up. It would be nice if you could talk to Tim. The housemother should have Tim on the first flight to Canyon City Airport, call this number, and his parents will pick him up. They are staying at their honeymoon cabin at the Royal Gorge, near the swing bridge."

Ray Albertson drove the limousine as far as Manito, where Avery picked up a nice, new rental car and the four drove to the hotel. Avery and Annabell took a room for only one night because they expected to find rooms wherever they wished to stop the next day. Ray and Evelan Albertson quickly said their goodbyes after asking Avery to be sure to meet then at the Canyon City Airport in eight days with the big plane and we will fly directly home. He had already made arrangements to leave the limousine at the rental agency at Colorado Springs.

Following Highway 115 was not as easy with the limousine, as there were many curves and a lot of road construction, so they were a little late arriving at the cabin and somewhat fatigued. As they had eaten at Canyon City, they watched the beautiful sunset from the porch of the cabin. The sun had just sunk beyond the edge of the canyon range when Tim's voice jubilant voice seemed to fill the room.

"Happy anniversary! I received your message and will be on the first flight. I will rent a jeep at the Springs. I'll bet that limousine was rather long to get around some of those mountain curves."

Around three the next afternoon, Tim arrived in his rental Jeep all ready for sightseeing, but his father said, "Better sit a spell, the altitude is much higher than you are used to at your school. It is still about sea-level at the floor of the gorge. There is a nice tram on the bottom of the gorge. It rolls down rails at an angle with all manner of safety devices and overhead cover as protection from falling rocks. I worked at the bottom some time that year we were married; at that time, workmen and material were lowered in a covered basket by a crane-operator. When I asked him how he knew when we got to the bottom, he said, "I listen for the crash!" I didn't believe him, but large Fourth of July fireworks were banned from the bridge!"

After an extra early evening meal, Albert and Evelan were sitting in the big porch-swing, holding hands ready to watch the sunset. Tim and his big, husky body was wedged between them. Evelan was making sure that their youngest son would not miss his first Colorado sunset.

Albert began to tell the story about why honeymoon cabin was built so far away from the rim of the canyon.

"From the time you were born, your mother has dreamed of this moment.

The depression had hit the country, and our country was trying to make jobs for as many as it could. An Easter Group convinced Washington that a bridge across the gorge with concessions on this side would attract tourists from all over the world and make even more employment.

"Manual-labor was very cheap that even draftsman and engineers were working at any manual-labor job until times got better.

"Well, good times were several years away and the money was always short for everyone in the country.

"Five years later, little Joe was four and into everything. He was the love of our hearts. I was working in Southeastern Colorado, running some survey lines. My beautiful lady, your mother, always traveled with me on those jobs, as there were many vacant tourist cabins because of the Great Depression. Everyone was so nice to your mother and little Joe. I can remember that first cabin. The first Sunday morning, we were invited by the landlady and her husband to attend church services. We met a lot of nice hardworking people, who were very devout. Little Joe was whisked into a class of children about his age.

"When the congregation stood to sing the opening hymn, your mother's voice sounded strong and clear. I was so proud of your mother, it still brings a tear.

"The tears did flow again when Joey's teacher told us at the dinner when he heard his mother's voice, he threw out his chest and said, 'That is my mother, she always sings to Dad and me!'

"We never missed a Sunday after that until the survey job was finished and we had to move away. Well, I started to tell you why our cabin is so far from the rim of the canyon....

"We were just pulling away from the crowd of our new friends. We had just been paid and didn't have to report to the new job for several days. Your mother said, "Let us go see the sunset at the gorge.' It is only about eighty miles northwest of us and almost on the way to our new post. Well, of course, I always responded to sound logic. We didn't arrive until almost dark. Not much had changed. The bridge had been closed off, because the road on the other side had not been completed to connect with another highway. It never started in over five years!

"There was a souvenir concession building operated by the resident park ranger and his family who also served sandwiches and coffee to few stragglers like ourselves. Those weren't too bad for your mother and me, but little Joe had to get by on toast, canned milk, and orange sucker that night!

"There was only one small unoccupied cabin pushed aside until it hung over the edge of the canyon almost a foot. We were told that we were welcome to stay overnight free, and that it was more save than driving back to Canyon City after dark!

"I always kept a camp-lantern in the truck for emergencies, so responding to even more logic, we lit the lantern and inspected the cabin by flickering light. The floor was clean, glasses in the two windows were slightly cracked, and there was no latch on the window-less door; other than that, the cabin seemed safe enough.

"However, there was no way to fasten the door shut.

"We were exhausted from the long drive that day. We placed Joe on the floor against the wall facing the street, thinking he would never move until first light the next morning. Even if he did, he would have to crawl over both of us, and we would wake up. Later, I was awakened by your mother's terrified scream, 'Joe is gone!'

"I lit the lantern while your mother went to alert the park rangers at the concession buildings. I was peering over the rim of the Canyon in the dim light of pre-dawn, thinking I could see some kind of movement at the foot of the first off-set about thirty feet down. I was almost in a state of panic hysterics, when here came your mother and the park ranger's wife with Joe in her arms! I tell you, Tim, your mother and I just sat down on a bench and blubbered! The ranger's wife, wise beyond her years, let our emotions subside, then told us this story.

"'I was just starting breakfast this morning when I heard a knock on the door. This is very polite little boy said, "Mother and Father are still asleep; may I have another slice of toast, please?" I started to fix the toast and thought how frightened you both would be when you discovered Little Joe was gone! Then I heard his mother scream and we started right down here.' The she finished her story with this statement ' Joe said, "I love my Mother and Dad very much, we have had a wonderful summer." And we all started tearing up again!"

Ray Albertson had intentionally delayed his story until the sunset was at its most beautiful aspects and his wife exclaimed, "There it is, just as it was sixty years ago! Oh, I wish we could preserve this moment somehow so everyone in this world could see it! Now watch how it sinks below the rim of the canyon and the shadows creep in!"

The trio sat in silence a few moments as they contemplated the wonders of the creatorship of their God. Then sobbing tears of sheer happiness drifted into the night air.

The moment may have been fleeting, but it would be remembered all their lives.

The next morning at breakfast, Time made two announcements.

"The jeep Cherokee is ready for a grand tour of this part of Colorado, you know. But, today, I would like to see if that cabin is still here, along with the concession building, and ride the train. Tomorrow is Sunday. I would like to visit the chapel where you and Mother were married."

The second announcement consisted of his wish to be a doctor of medicine. His mother gasped, "Oh, they grow up so quickly!"

His father's reply was a quick study of his personality.

"There is a fine school and hospital at McCook, Nebraska. That school and hospital is well established in the arts as well as sciences. Your conduct and skills in your chosen profession depend very much on your social skills as you walk this pathway of life. You are from good stock. Culture doesn't necessarily dance along the pathway of life, but your life will be much more pleasant if it does."

The trip stopped at the concession building and the park ranger led them fifty feet down the roadway and there sat the most disreputable-looking cabin, just as Evelan Albertson remembered it. There were the cracked windows and the plank door without a latch. His camera in hand, Tim took extra pictures of the cabin, the door, the windows and then of his mother and father. Lastly, he asked his father to take a picture of him and the ranger, and a shot of the steep slope behind the cabin.

Tim was beginning to realize the near panic his parents must have experienced that morning so long ago, and how difficult it must have been to relate the story of Joe, their first-born, and understand the closeness between his father and Joe.

They had eaten breakfast with the ranger and his wife when Tim asked about the chapel. They were told the services were at ten that morning.

Watching the radiance of the expression on the faces of his mother and father as they sang their praise to their God, Tim began to worry about his own worthiness. Little did he realize it was his willingness and determination that was to lead him the rest of his long life.

The trio was invited to the dinner served that afternoon, consisting of breads of all varieties it seemed, Graham, wheat, rice wheat, oatmeal, and huge bowls of jellies and jams. A haunch of antelope had been barbequed. There were pies of apple, quince, blueberry, and several wild strawberries....

An elderly gentleman gave the blessing, saying, "The young ladies will be serving us today. The young gentlemen will do the cleaning because we have declared this Mother's Day!"

After sixty years, very few in the neighborhood were there when Ray Albertson worked on building the bridge in his youth. The couple dearest to their heart were Bill and Edna Grissom. They stood up with Ray and Evelan at their wedding. They served as advisors in determining the location of the honeymoon cabin, becoming its caretakers after overseeing its building.

Tim took his parents and the Grissoms in the leased Jeep Cherokee for a trip about the countryside, stopping at several mines where Bill had, in his younger years, mined Colorado hard coal! The last stop before lunch was a gold mine, where Bill had made his first strike that had lasted almost fifteen years before the vein ran out. After that, he had leased it to a group to run as an authentic Old Tim Gold Mine near the entrance to the Gorge Bridge Park, as a concession.

A contract signed by the members of the group provided that they carry liability insurance required of anyone who entered the premises, maintain safe condition in the mine, and submit to the yearly Colorado mines inspection. This contract shall relieve the Grissoms of all responsibility. In the future, the Grissoms were to receive ten percent gross from both mining and concession.

The contract also contained several more provisions covering compliance of contract, state and federal taxes, etc., absolving the Grissoms of all responsibility in the operation of the mine. The contract is not transferable during the life of this conract.

In the early years of the contract, the revenue was almost nil. After the depression was over and more people began to travel, Colorado started to advertise the beauty of its parks on its road-maps. The revenue from the mine concession increased during summer and fall and to nil again during the winter month, but with the income from the caretaker's job and as an occasional hunting and-fishing guide, the Grissoms had lived better than average and settled into retirement.

The pilot, Avery Graham, and Annabell had driven to the Royal Gorge on a Sunday to visit and ride the tram to the bottom of the gorge. They were able to enjoy the sunset with the Albertsons. Avery had set up his camera hoping to preserve the sunset. Annabell had taken video pictures of all the little towns. She had collected enough memorabilia that insured them many pleasant copy evenings on their return home. She managed to get some footage of the sunset, which she hoped would be unbelievably good. She had been told many times the light was never just quite right!

Every one's schedule for their vacations had slipped by so quickly they were reluctant to leave the next morning.

Bill and Edna Grissom, the caretakers, would clean the cabin and lease the rooms as overnight lodging to visitors of the gorge. This year, they were including breakfast of hotcakes, sausages, and coffee, because the park rangers were not opening early enough. It had taken almost all of last year for Bill Grissom to obtain his Colorado hotel and café license because he wanted to accommodate the occasional hunter. This year, there had been a ban placed on all the smaller parks, as a safety measure. He would be able to guide the hunters in other areas and board them in the cabin, which is an unhandy arrangement.

Avery and Annabell left early to return their car to the leasing agency in Colorado Springs. Tim would leave after them. He would leave the Jeep at the agency in Canyon City. Ray and Evelan would leave next and pick them all up in the limousine. The two younger men driving arrived in Denver well before dark at a hotel Ray had made reservations just before leaving the Gourd.

Ray Albertson used the phone in the limousine to call the home office in Omaha to get the progress report of the Paradise Village models and how, if the surveying was finished, and about all else- the long range weather report, and if son, Joe, had made any core-drillings for the stability of foundations. Satisfied with all the reports, Ray turned the phone over to Avery Graham and said, "Here, find out if our pack mule is full of oats and ready to carry us home. I think we should stop at McCook and see our friends, the Goldsmith girls and their parents and how they are doing in their school.

Their stay at the Best Western Hotel, however, was a businessman's delight. There was a special, large, well-lighted room with every imaginable office machines, with charming, brilliant young operators should they be needed. However, if the business deal requires core security from prying eyes, such as price discounts, that security would also be provided by the hotel.

Should a sales executive and his group of sales-representatives have a store whose sales were down, and he called for a sales promotion in that store, the young ladies in the business office could be put together a very credible sales promotion using their expertise. It could also be a fashion promotion for a department store, a grocery chain, men's clothing.

The promotion the hotel group was most proud of, the one that drew record attendance and sales, was for a farm implement dealer in a city out on the plains that also had a Best Western Hotel with a business accommodation room. They left a skeletal crew in Denver as a backup, rented two small vans, and planned their strategy by cell-phone on the way to Wheat City.

The last evening in Denver, the two families rested briefly after their long ride from the Royal Gorge vicinity. They were dining leisurely in the dining room of the Best Western Hotel when the waiter spoke up, informing everyone that there would be dancing that evening in the grand ballroom at nine.

The ladies thought that an hour or so would be a fine way to end a very pleasant vacation and spent over an hour dancing before they retired.

The next morning found the group several thousand feet in the clear blue sky, winging their way with the pilot, Avery Graham, at the controls, his wife Annabell as co-pilot, sitting proudly across from him in a sharp new uniform.

Everyone was to learn about this young lady.

She had been in the United States Women's Air Force during the war, but she had never mentioned it to anyone! For several years now, she had gone to flying school to regain her license and captain's bars that she thought she would never need after she left the services. Now, she was hoping doing so would help hold her marriage together. Oh, what tangled webs we weave! At that very moment, Avery was bursting with pride in Annabell for having the stamina to stay with the project. He, too, had been so lonely on some of those long ferry trips taking a plane to an owner. At the moment, all he could say was, "We sure had fun this trip, didn't we?"

On their arrival at McCook airport, the owner of the hotel had his van waiting to take them to his hotel and bring everyone up on any news at the hospital. There had been several auto wrecks and injuries that had kept the doctors all busy last week. John Smith and Erma had married. They were living at the dorm for married students and going to school and working part time in the records department.

The baby, Bobby, was fed a bottle with the special formula (as prescribed by the Kansas City doctor) by Joyce Goldsmith as a special assignment, with the approval of all the doctors, though Mrs. North was not quite sure it could be done without complications because that girl needed more rest when she started school. It was a valid reason, but it was over-ruled.

Little Ella, the undernourished baby, was going well on a special formula. She gained almost two pounds. Her mother was not convinced her own lack of a proper diet had been the trouble.

We were given to understand the lab had to discover that the sores on little Eve's body had come from the rock crusher dust where her father worked, but so far had been unable to identify the prehistoric virus or a cure because it took time to produce a culture sample. It had been proven by cultures from the sores of her father and Eve that were shown to be identical. Samples of biopsies were sent to other labs for their advice and expertise.

The doctors were reluctant to speak with the media, who might mis-interpret and start panic unnecessarily in the city and the state.

Tamala Goldsmith had to spend much more time in changing into protective clothing; little Eve Brandon, her mother, was in isolation, too. Mrs. North, director of volunteers, was heard to mutter under her breath, Tam is too sensitive to be a good nurse!" Time will tell which one would be the happiest.

Tamala had found some sturdy, washable material covered with pictures in the park, out of which she had made herself and tiny Eve smocks and Eve began talking about which ones were her father and mother. Tam felt at the moment that Eve's family ties were secure.

The Ray Albertson group dined again at the hotel. They were in the air once more on the way to Omaha by eleven thirty that morning, having learned that the rock crusher near McCook was shutting down indefinitely. He wanted to see if his son, Joe, had contracted for any crushed stone like that in any of their buildings thinking ahead this firsthand if the models of the whole lay-out was just like he had been picturing in his mind while they were in Colorado.

Joe came in that weekend with a lot of encouraging news. The co-op wanted to build a huge all like building that would house a large men's clothing, a women's clothing, and a large pharmacy, all with wide aisles to accommodate the electric wheelchairs. The co-op farm machinery would be some distance away because there was need for a lot of room for those large combines.

Joe continued, "Dad, I think that we should own those wheelchairs. We can get a factory-trained man to manage a building for us and keep the fumes from charging the batteries out of the main building."

"Sounds like a good idea," his father replied. "That is why we will have such a large percentage of young energetic knowledgeable nurses working in unison. As the residents grow older, we shall need those nurses to keep the residents active and in good health, without ever being intrusive in our relationship with the residents.

"That independent group that has been working with McCook Hospital, I liked what I saw taking place in that hospital. I believe the principle will work in our situation. Joe, how soon do you suppose the models of the whole complex will be ready? I will contract Mr. Gleeson, who is in charge of that independent advisory group at the hospital, if he might have some suggestions. We just might be able to install some cabinets, work-tables, and bed in the ICU. That would be time and energy savers, instead of having to remove and start over. Joe, if you're building something this complicated, we could avoid it if we organized before we start. The time you have to start doing tasks over again to make right is when personnel start making even more errors because of frustration and confusion."

Ray Albertson continued talking to his eldest son, Joe.

"There should be at least eighteen apartments with a wide hallway between them running east and west. This will mean eighteen apartments with a north exposure and eighteen apartments facing the south.

"The kitchen building would be located just west of the west end of the main building. That is the picture I drew in my mind just talking to John Smith that one time. He was kind of overwhelmed at the thought of the size of the project.

"The way the community has endorsed the project, we should be free of debt in the ten of fifteen years.

"Our firm is to sublet the plumbing, electric, and furniture, and those contractors will be pushing us so they can order their material. Another thing: We have to be careful these sub-contractors don't install any shoddy material like poor bathrooms fixtures of poor glaze that stain easily, which then have to be changed in two years. All that sure leads to big turnover of housekeepers who have to do double work trying to keep things clean and sanitary.

"Disgruntled labor of the subcontractors can affect the general contractor. Over the years, you learn who not to deal with!"

Ray Albertson had analyzed, in a few brief moments, some of the situations that could cause the organization trouble and expense and how to avoid situations before they had the opportunity to start.

Joe Albertson had spent a great deal of time in the model making department. He had men whose many skills include making reproduction models to a scale of one inch equaling about half the size of the structure in question. To arrive at workable model of kitchen and bathroom appliances, the draftsmen must have the exact position of all pipes and electrical conduits. At the same time, they must allow for accessibility so workmen could install, remove, or replace an appliance.

Knowing the cooperative attitude of the people in the small towns of Kansas, Joe Albertson and his wife visited the churches in Paradise-Village, looking for any storm-cloud of dissension that might have been overlooked in everyone's enthusiasm that their village was on the verge of becoming prosperous and enjoy some of the things other people considered big city advantages like sewer lines, paved streets with curb and gutter, larger drinking water-lines that do not rust and has better water pressure, lots of shade trees, full-time street employees, as well as trash and garbage trucks with regular scheduled pick-up, and well-developed recycling system.

They expected well-laid property lines and new housing in a price range that would not be a burden to the purchaser.

All of these made Ray Albertson shudder to think how forlorn Paradise Village would look when the construction was finished. The town-that-had-become-a-city almost overnight, but he knew the skilled workers would follow their trades when his son Joe moved on to even larger construction. He had seen it happen before and he didn't want it to happen in the very town he had chosen to spend his late elderly retirement!

Rat Albertson and son, Joe, met with city officials to find a suitable building where they might display the models of the apartment building, the ICU, grounds maintenance building, the place where the building to conduct maintenance of electric wheel-chairs.

Ray Albertson had worked out a program he thought might be of interest to all. He talked to John Smith and Erma, who was now Mrs. John Smith, by cell phone, and had made arrangement for the graduating class of nurses, Dr. Webber and his wife, and Mrs. Clara North. That should be about a full load for the van. Each was asked to give a brief speech on their avocation. It was also suggested some Paradise Village residents be invented into their homes, to expound more effectively, under actual home situations, on their questions.

At a town meeting with the Albertsons, it was decided to use the civic auditorium for everyone to meet to display the model of the buildings and equipment, as there were plenty of long tables and chairs. Should the weather be inclement, the barbecue could be served inside.

The beef was being supplied by Bar-K Ranch of Albert and Sarah Goldsmith and prepared by their ranch cook and his helpers.

At this point, Ray Albertson was beginning to be impatient to get started on the foundation. He knew he wasn't this anxious in his first contract. He stopped to realize that on the first contract, he was the one who had made all the decisions, planning, and carried the full load of responsibility. This time his son had assumed a huge portion of the responsibility while his father and mother were on their vacation. Joe had not bothered his father with details while Ray was on vacation. Joe was a good son. From the day he went to work for his father, he had kept his eyes and ear open and his mouth shut, observing everything his father was doing and the results thereof.

Ray and Joe next visited the local newspaper office, having set the date of September 16, 2000- it being on a Saturday- for the county and city people to see the models on display. They met with an editor who had been rather outspoken in his editorials about the lack of care in many homes about the country. They would not want to deprive him of an opportunity to see for himself how they plan to care for the elderly, which they considered would be tantamount to a disservice.

"We need the media on our side. Let us go right now and mend a fence that isn't really broken yet. We should call on him and see how he reacts if we offer him some of our advertisement. He may turn out to be our best friend... . By the way, who does he play golf with?" When told that the editor and his wife usually played golf on Sunday afternoon with the mayor and his wife, Ray exclaimed, "There you are!" and reached for his cell phone.

Ray spoke briefly with the editor for an appointment. He asked for advice on the lay0out of the exhibit of the models and the barbecue. Turning to his son, he said, "Joe we need to find out what day the advertisement in the mall. If people read it too early, they lay it aside and forget to make plans to be there, then they have to cancel other plans. If delivery is too late, it is obvious the show is over!"

The next day, Ray and his son called on the edit, Alexander, who, when told the plan was to cover the whole county, offered to turn out a special edition, along with more flyer adds covering a few suggestions in the size of print. However, Mr. Albertson and Joe's names were not to appear in print larger than pica size. It did include an order for bound manuscript that contained the schedule when certain phases of the work were projected to be finished, depending on the city providing more than adequate underground water lines and sewer disposal plant. This would require perhaps a deferral and state civic loan for small towns and cities. These loans usually ran for about twenty-five years; it could be extended under certain circumstances, and the interest was quite low. With the expected increase in building of new homes for the people who would be working at the co-ops, there should not be a huge increase in the mill levy. I think every lady who has emptied a pan of dishwater out the back kitchen door will benefit from this for years.

The Albertson construction company had noted elevation and grade stakes while they were checking the boundary lines of the real estate.

"We are willing to lay approved high-pressure non-rust water lines on our property to connect with your lines of the same approved material. We will also place fire-hydrants at approved locations on our property in our high-rise buildings. We feel that will save the city when it finances additions to the water and sewage plants. Using the very best approved materials will save everyone a lot of maintenance inconvenience that over the years will be appreciated by the city and elderly who will reside in the apartments.

"With 216 apartments, we anticipate there will be a tremendous amount of both fresh and waste-water used every day."

The almost two pages of conversation with the editor, Mr. Alexander, was more or less, if need be, to alert him that the whole project was not just fun and games. Instead, it would require diligent cooperation from the city if it expected to reap much benefit from the project as a whole, and who better than the local editor could, through his brilliantly written columns, bring and hold unity among the city officials?

The morning of September 16, 2000, was clear. A slight breeze from the Southwest was heralding a pleasant day. The Bar K Rand cook and his helpers arrived in the early morning hours with the pre-barbecued beef. It had been pit-barbecuing for several days, as attested by eight-inch by ten-inch photos hanging all over the sides of the truck showing just how it was accomplished and how it had been kept warm until its arrival from the ranch ten miles north-west of Stockton, Kansas. Six of the fifty-pound packets of pre-boned meat had been removed from their wrappings and placed in huge pans, their juice now warming up on the special trailer, until the tantalizing odors started to drift into the very center of town!

The fiesta dancers and their escorts, dressed in their traditional flamboy-ant uniforms, were dancing on platform to the music of their native country.

Their leader announced they would be their guides through the displays and passed out the literature.

The displays first showed the completed building and the proposed formal garden, followed by how completed entire floor would look with the furniture.

The kitchens and the combination bath and laundry room drew more at-tention than the rest of the apartment, because every known safety precaution had been taken to prevent injury and falls.

"The housekeeping services could be used part time, but we suggest that every one after age sixty-five should have a nurse who lives in, or three that rotated every eight hours because these people are trained to watch for signs of illness. And you know your children and grand-children would worry less knowing someone was keeping an eagle eye on then."

The town residents began drifting, following the odor of the barbecue. Most were walking in from their homes, to leave parking spaces for those from the neighboring towns who would soon be arriving. "How thoughtful," murmured Ray Albertson.

The early arrivals were met by some of fiesta dancers, into the building, after they had been handed the very neatly bound manuscript describing the models. Every detail was in terms that the concern for the elderly was uppermost in the minds of the designers.

This group, probably numbering two hundred and fifty, was very inquisitive about every detail of the living arrangements and of the cost, of course. Many were families, with their eldest children urging their parents to put their names on the prospective list now and be the first to move in after the building was finished, well at least a year from the time.

After two hours, there was a long line of people standing at the door. All were let in, manuscripts in hand. After some time, the building had become crowded. Some who stepped outside for a breath of fresh air saw the barbecue, followed by others, until the tables were full and lines were forming at the second group tables. The fiesta dancers were scurrying about clearing tables, some even singing catchy songs in their language. There were no squeaking loudspeakers, just good people having fun! This was characteristic of most small towns.

The winds of fate were blowing strongly for John Smith and his new wife, Erma. That evening, as the day drew to a close and the sun seemingly sunk into the prairie of western Kansas, Joe announced to his father that thirty-six apartments had been contracted for, thanks to the wives of Jim smith and the auto agency salesmen.

"They have worked very hard. They deserve some recognition," said Ray, "You see to it soon."

All federal, state, and local permits by Ray Albertson Construction Company had been checked by the legal department at the home office in Omaha; each was placed in each one's respective file holders with four-page cover sheets signed by the attorney-in-charge of the office. These sheets pointed out where diligence was required to stay in compliance when installing certain equipment. Copies of these permits were to be placed in the office of the maintenance department of the apartments.

Ray Albertson had, for a number of years, kept his office in a huge lowboy trailer. His private office was not large, but it included his personal chief office manager, Mr. Kyle, who was well versed in handling huge amounts of every kind of construction material, to be stored in the trailer and delivered after ten days, when the storage cost became quite expensive. Mr. Kyle had a number of accountants and clerks who made sure every item on the invoice were in the loads, be it a kitchen stove or a keg of nails. The home office people had become quiet expert in balancing the arrival time of most materials.

Ray Albertson asked Joe when the forms for the foundations would be stacked and when the excavating crew their machinery were ready to start. Those east-west runs are very long. We sure don't have to correct an error after the concrete is poured. That sure would be an expensive basement if we have to do it over. Do you know who is carrying the risk insurance on our employees?"

Joe answered almost to everything without referring to his notebook.

He then told his father that he had contracted with a company any number from twenty-five to twenty-seven[nbbande7] portable sanitary bath-houses that would be clean and fresh every morning. "There were twelve here today!"

Ray replied, "Sorry, I did overlook that."

While Ray and Joe would be busy with the first of the earth-moving crews and where best to store the back-fill earth- that it could be done with less energy expended, perhaps we should look into the local editor, Mr. Alexander. He had called in two new young health columnists who were to write precautions everyone should follow for maintaining a safe health schedule. Knowing the housewives of the county and their thrift, Mr. Alexander included a cardboard file each week. The two columnists, a married couple, wrote so intriguingly that they soon began to receive letter asking questions to be in the next paper- the next day they hoped- but being a weekly paper, that was impossible. In a month time, with a new state and federal license and three additional press men, it became a daily and just barely making postal delivery of the county, under the banner called *City Express*.

Our next stop should the local café, hungry men have to eat you know!

Hap and Marion drifted into town and set up in an abandoned dance hall nearly twenty years ago, when the new highway was being built. They had stayed on after the highway was finished, because Marion said, "Hap, I am tired of running every two month. I want to stay here and raise a family. We have made good friends here. We can make a living here, I think. Not great, but enough."

So they became residents of the town. Sometimes, Hap found work for the city; sometimes during harvest time, he made enough to improve the café, and the children always came from the school. They had a safe refuge here. Our children now have deep roots here.

Hap and Marion just about knew what Joe wanted when he walked in that morning and ordered coffee. There was no one else at the counter when Hap waited on Joe.

Marion, in new fresh uniform, hair newly permed, leaned back the pie and cake counter and said, "Hi, I am Marion, the other half of the Lonesome Pine Café! The last time I saw you was about covered with dirt and dust and more brash kid I ever saw. Are you pushing this Smith job now?" The bantering continued "you ate a steak, mashed potatoes, and where you had room for a whole cherry pie, no one ever knew."

Joe said, "I am still with Dad. We are going to try out a different method excavating; a six cubic yard bite will be elevated into a truck. This is about the size job needed because the machine is so large. I understand the whole basement is to be storm shelter also! That means the ceiling needs extra reinforcing. The main building sure will require am immense amount of concrete. The free-standing ICU will only be one story and basement. We also hope to have the contract for the big new co-op grocery, both a men and women clothing department, and a huge pharmacy mall contract.

"Those truck drivers will have their house trailers parked at the camp so they have a place to rest. They will be running from can't in the morning to can't see a night and usually eat on the fly or waiting in line for a load. They are good ethical men, paid by the load and mileage. Several of the drivers' wives are as expert drivers as their husbands, and often drive while the man eats. Most of these men will be pulling the big three trailer freight on regular runs of 350 and 400-mile runs. Many fail to keep their driving log-book up-to-date or are stopped by the highway patrol for traffic or lights violations, and are soon back to the hauling dirt. It is just a matter of self-discipline and the traveling public who hide behind those three long loads, and then pop out into on-coming traffic with his wife and three kids, and there is no place to go. A few incidents like that and the driver is so filled and three kids, and there is no place to go. A few incidents like that and the driver is so filled with stress he becomes an inept driver, missing road warning signs, failing to shift down on hills to keep the same speed. The next stop is back to hauling dirt!

"Well, we didn't move any dirt yesterday and today started at the Lonesome Pine Café, where twenty eight and ten trucks were to stand by until noon; should any truck stall, the line of trucks would never slow down. Those numbers could never be used again until every truck had been a stand-by for four hours.

"The reinforcing rods and other materials needed for the foundation would not arrive for several days, but the plan shows the special wooden forms for the concrete, complete with window, entrance and ventilation openings, water, sewer, electrical- these openings need special sealing to prevent concrete seeping into the openings becoming a part of the foundation!

With a Booster Club like Mr. Alexander, the editor, all the managers of the various departments of the co-op and all those now working with Hap and Marion at the Lonesome Pine Café, Ray and Joe Albertson with all their experience in construction makes one wonder if maybe we haven't neglected someone back in McCook, Nebraska, like Bobby, Jacson, Ella, Elmer, Pettie, and last but not least little Eve and her family.

Upon our arrival at McCook Hospital, we found Clara North setting at her desk, a cool wet cloth pressed to her temples. Half dazed with pain, she raised her head and said, "You are…?"

When told her I was a friend of Joyce and Tamala Goldsmith, she said, "Oh yes, now I remember you."

I asked her if she was in great pain and she replied, "This is the worse attack I ever had and it came on so sudden."

Not knowing just what to do, I helped her to the couch, head slightly raised.

Then I pressed the call button and said, "Mayday! Mayday! Clara North is ill here in her office! She needs help!"

Then I heard slamming of doors after which three nurses rushed in. Two rushed over to the couch while the third pressed the button and called, "Code blue! Code blue! Clara's office!" In moments, nurses were pushing a gurney, heart monitor, oxygen, and several other machines. I had no idea what they were! I just moved into a corner and stood in awe at the efficiency of the group. Dr. Webber and Dr. Wilson arrived and was handed the readings as they came off the machines. I heard Dr. Webber say, "We need another scan. It could be a tumor; however, with that much pain, a blocked artery should not be ruled out. We need an MRI scan as soon as possible. We want to prevent stroke, and we sure don't need a clot breaking loose, either. Get the MRI then into intensive care then call me. I shall be here all night if need be. I want to call her husband myself right now."

Thus, the author, wandering desolately in the big empty lobby, where Joyce Goldsmith spoke a few words of comfort and taking me gently by the arm, guided me into the chapel. We sat in back, in the half darkened room gently speaking, trying to calm my stress. In a few minutes, tears began to stream down my cheeks. Then Joyce said, "Think of the tears of anguish our savior's mother shed *that day* at the foot of the cross."

When Joyce spoke of tears of anguish, I raised and gazed about the candle-lighted chapel. It was filled with kneeling nurses in their white uniforms, offering prayers for the welfare of Clara North. I had no knowledge of the time the group had been kneeling; for myself, my knees were starting to ache and I shifted around a bit. Then I felt a hand on my shoulder. Glancing around, I saw there was no one on the bench except me. Joyce was in the row ahead of me! Then, a low melodious voice seemed to come from the air about and above me saying, "All the prayers were heard and the lord has many, many tasks for Clara North, here in this very hospital. She is recovering in her room. She will be weak and her recovery will seem slow to her, but to Joyce and Tamala caring for her, they will earn many things that will be remembered for centuries."

The group of nurses arose and sang praise to the Lord, walked to Clara North's room where Dr. Webber met then and allowed only one of their choosing to talk to Clara that night, while he explained to the rest of the group what had been going on. He began by saying, "I take no credit for any of this what-so-ever. We were taking the x-ray of the tumor and as we watched, it started to shrink, we watched until it had completely disappeared. I think we have seen a miracle!"

After several days of complete rest and the nurses measuring out the prescribed vitamins and a very good balanced diet, the stress seemed to leave the muscles relaxed, the constant massaging managed to keep the muscles strong and blood circulating.

Two special nurses were assigned to assist Clara on short walks and later on longer walks about the halls until her strength had been regained. The Miracle Lady!

The author was allowed a ten minute tea time visit with Clara North during her first week of convalescence. Those moments were like drops of pure gold. She spoke of her church and the pleasures It had brought to her and those who were friends and neighbors. I do not recall hearing her ever saying a disrespectful word to anyone.

I remember her speaking of the Garden of Eden as if were her very own. The beautiful, fantastic flowers, every color of the rainbow. How some were so delegate, a breath would destroy it. She spoke of the flowers sometimes as thought they were living people and what she would do caring for them.

She spoke of the beautiful flowering fruit trees, and how most need care too. Then she spoke of the disobedience of Adam and Eve, with tears streaming down her cheeks, how she would have tried to persuade them from eating from the tree of life. One could really believe had she been here, she would have made our president world quite different.

The author cherishes those seven tea moments all his lifetime. Clara North's face, though no longer drawn in pain, was, however, sometimes drawn in sorrow. I remember entering room one morning and finding her weeping inconsolably, and saying, "If only I had been there, I might have been of some help and comfort! Dr. Wilson's new mother patient had lost her first-born. Oh, that empty-armed mother!" Clara moaned.

A nurse came by and said, "Dr Wilson had ordered a sedative," and she administered a shot.

The tea-tray sat untouched and gone cold. An aid came by and added the tray to her cart.

I sat there staring at Clara North's smooth clear face, until a shirt-change nurse came and I spent an hour or so in the chapel. After that, I wandered aimlessly back to the hotel.

The next morning, I was awakened by a mournful song of a prairie plover calling killdeer, killdeer, killdeer, as it floated gracefully past my window.

This only reminded me my own happy-unhappy prairie roots. Then, I wondered where the meadow larks with their merry rill could be. Thinking about this, I went down to breakfast. The waitress in freshly-starched uniform greeted me with, "Oh, my, you look glum this morning!"

I shot back, "Where are all the meadow larks?"

"Oh," she said, "the prairie pasture land was growing full of a thorny thistle, and the best time to spray was right at hatching time of our prairie birds that lay next on the ground! The meadow lark mothers became frightened and fled the next, and the baby birds were drenched. Now the killdeer mother tucked her head under her wing and pulled her feathers down tight over her babies and protected most of them. That's what the federal agriculture man told us. He said the spray was pulled off the market as soon as the damage was discovered. Can't blame the birds, the wing blew the seed in."

I decided right at that moment that this was one subject we would not discuss with Clara North at least not until she had a complete recovery from her present illness. Again, I was in another dilemma. I felt I owe a degree of conventionality to Clara North because of our Tea Time discussions. On the other hand, I couldn't ask the waitress to curb her story on a subject that was common knowledge.

Approaching the hospital somewhat apprehensively the next morning for our ten-minute Tea Time, Clara North greeted me with a cherry "Good morning!" and asked if it was her turn to pour the tea, "If you wish, I will butter the toast. Do you like blueberry jelly?"

Our Tea Time passed all too quickly. Clara was full of happy news. John Smith and his wife had visited the evening before with a beautiful card, ice cream, and news about their classes. They, too, had brightened and enriched the life of our miracle lady. They had at least four more years of classes before they could start on their life goal of helping the elderly.

We didn't feel we should intrude on the lives of Bobby, Jason, Ella, Elmer, Pettie, and little Eve until we had an opportunity to talk with the very busy Goldsmith girls with their full-time classes and special assignments the doctors had given them, to help pay their way through school, although they had promised they would devote full time the first six months of classes! Knowing the dedication of the Goldsmith ladies, we just hoped they would take some social part of their time in college.

Knowing the sage of McCook, Clara North, had this in her mind ever since she met the Goldsmith ladies, as she repeated the saying, "All work and no play makes Jack a dull boy." All this brings one to wonder if, perhaps, Clara North may have some regrets of how she handled her own social affairs. However, her skill during the snobbery of the waitress and the mix of the English and Italian menu that saved Tamala some embarrassment seemed to believe so. Also, at the same private dinner, when Clara's sister and grandson intruded on them, Clara handled that in a very clever manner without embarrassment, seen also in the way she side stepped dancing with her grandson.

We continued our Tea Time for two more weeks. Then, one morning, the two nurses who had always attended to Clara North in her walks around the hospital rose gardens asked if we would be free to assist Clara North with her wheelchair in the mall. The trio wanted to do some shopping and needed someone husky to push the chair in the heavy crowd and help with the packages.

The next morning, we all assembled at the hospital lobby before the hospital van carried all of us safely to the mall and promised to return for us when we called. Well, we pushed the wheelchair itno the mall right into the arms of the mall welcoming committee.

By this time, the media had spread the news of the Miracle lady.

The two nurses stepped in front of Clara North, protesting that her health was still too frail to speak for a very short time. They explained they were bound by their profession and that of the doctor's that nothing loud speech or music, or questions might disturb their out patients. The nurses continued: If you will give us questions that we deep appropriate, in writing- turning to the mall manager, the nurse asked him, "Do you have *Just a Closer Walk with Thee and Abide with Me?* If you do, please have them used all verses very softy while the media is writing their questions."

After the first notes floated from the instruments, two low melodious voices drifted from the gathered mall spectators and the two young ladies, formerly of the Bar Z (Z) Cattle and Wheat ranch, now in training at McCook Hospital, stepped over beside the other two nurses.

The songs finished, the two ladies Joyce and Tamala Goldsmith gazed about the mesmerized faces of the media and mall spectators and raised their hands palms outward as though to prevent any further advance from the crowd. Not a sound or movement came from the people. Tamala, speaking in the same low voice, said, "My sister and I are very surprised, as are Clara and her two nurses, by the suddenness of this. We all feel honored that all of you wanted to pay your respect to Clara North. Her appearance today was to purchase some new clothing to brighten her convalescence. Her nurses just informed me she is due back at the hospital before lunch, and rest and complete physical this afternoon. We are now rather pressed for time; hand us your questions, and if they are appropriate, I, Tamala Goldsmith, will read them to Clara and that way, you will have both on your recorder.

The reporters had chosen one of their members to speak for then. He stepped forward and said, "In the midst of our reporting, we forget to conduct ourselves properly. Thank you for the intervention before we got out of order. I have collected only three questions, one from your local paper here in McCook.

Question number 1: Does God observe all our thoughts and actions?

Question number 2: Who is the true God?

Question number 3: What are the attributes of God?

Clara North's answers are on page 88.

Clara's response to question number 1:

I believe He is aware of all our actions and thoughts, but does not intervene sometimes, wishing us to realize and rectify our action and attitudes.

Her response to question number 2:

God is a spirit; no man has seen his face. He has no physical body. He is our creator and creator of all things!

Her response to question number 3:

His awesome power. (Exodus 9:16)

His wisdom. (Romans 11:33)

His Love. (Deuteronomy 32:04)

Clara North leaned back in her chair, drew a deep breath, and said, "I am very thankful someone found me that day at the office and knew how to summon help quickly. I believe someone of great power from heaven guided then to my rescue. I also believe this meeting today was arranged and guided by His awesome power, His wisdom, and his love, and in some way, will change all our lives.

"Clara," said Tamala, "our time grows short. We must do our shopping and return to the hospital."

The crowd dispersed and our group entered the women's apparel aisles.

"I wish to buy two dark evening gowns and two others in the lighter colors. I am depending on you, nurses, to select those with the latest style and material." Turning to Joyce Goldsmith, Clara said in a whisper, "What I really need is a lot of waterproof under-garments. Will you slip away and select them for me, please? Here are the sizes."

Sizes, Joyce thought as she excused herself form the group, *these are all for tiny children! Clara has another project. There is no end to her giving herself and her treasures. I shall see if we might help her with her project.*

Joyce Goldsmith had asked me to push the large shopping cart, now filled with square plain-wrapped packages that Joyce had asked the salesgirl to mark the price, and we had been given enough large shopping bags with handles to be used at the checkout stand. We struggled through the now-increasing crowd to the rotunda. Where we found Clara North, her two nurses, and Tamala drinking cups of golden tea with a platter of Swiss cookies, quite generous in size, I might add, and I help myself to one! A waitress poured us tea in quaint cups. As we sipped our tea, we listened to Clara tell us stories about her childhood on the plains of Nebraska and the hardships of the Indian women and the women settlers. I made mental note to ask her more of those times so very long ago.

The van driver and he wanted a thermos of tea. Joyce and Tamala began to fight and look at their watches. Somehow, between the driver and me, we loaded all of Clara's purchases, Clara and her wheelchair, and the four young ladies into the vanm and managed the two-mile run back to the hospital. For myself, I was very tired and so were all the ladies. Clara's shoulders were beginning to droop, too.

The nurses on second shift were waiting; they hustled Clara into a warm bath and, on advice of Dr. Webber, her physical was postponed until the next afternoon. However, he wanted a stress-test before and after her warm bath the day of her return pulse, blood test, and MRI which were all done before her evening meal.

Doctor's Webber and Wilson and their nurses were just starting to go over Clara's x-rays and other papers before continuing, when Dr. Webber asked if there were any objection to having the two Goldsmith girls on this physical today. Hearing no "Nays," he asked that they be brought to the examination room and that they were to enter singing the same songs they were singing yesterday at the mall. Turning to the nurse, he asked her "to watch a lesion near the temple as the girls enter, please. I shall try and snap a picture."

Clara had lain quietly listening to all the procedures. When they were over, everything was blank not a thing had changed! Then, Clara spoke in her clear, gentle voice: "You cannot test our lord."

With those three simple words, Clara gently reminded everyone in the room once again of the wisdom of God without injury to one's ego. "I believe I have been twice-blessed by all of you by your loving and caring for my welfare these many days."

A rather bewildered but much wiser group filed from the examination room that afternoon.

The nurses began tidying up their work-stations. Joyce and Tamala Goldsmith began bringing me up-to-date information about little Eve and Bobby, their two special charges.

The roof of Bobby's mouth had been grafted in and growing and expanding with the rest of his face, his upper left clip filled in and expanding as expected. He is now almost eight months old and feeding from a bottle, the terrible pain of the operation now forgotten.

One morning while talking with the Goldsmith ladies, we mentioned something about the rock-dust, or rather the absence of it in the air, and that

I might go out and see the location of the rock-crusher some time on my strolls about the city. I was advised to stay away from that section of town especially if the wind was blowing. The city passed an ordinance that everyone should wear masks until the ordinance was lifted and all danger had passed.

Preferring my cozy room at the hotel to the jail-cell, I never went near that section of town. I did, however, obtain a certified face-mask and joined the rest of the city populace for pure air to breathe. To tell the truth, I never was able to understand what people were saying under those masks.

We continued checking with Clara North. On her regular Tea Time, Clara was not a prude, but she did demand some decorum in speech, dress, and deportment. Not in so many words, but there was going to be a quick straightening of my tie or a phase[nbbande8] some materials need pressing more often than others. Never anything to make one feel embarrassed, Clara was always ready with a list of books for me to pick at the library for her. The following days, we discussed every sentence in those books. What was the author trying to convey to the reader his own feelings or that of the characters in the book? And what words made the thoughts almost optically visual as one scanned the sentences and paragraphs?

Clara North became so intense in her interest in both old authors' books and those written by authors of our generation, that we put my trusty recorder into recording every word spoken in each session that winter. By studying them in my hotel room each night, I was able to remember most of it.

I had been almost eighteen months since we left Paradise Village, the village that was once a struggling farming community now being transformed from the dreams of John Smith and his new bride, into a true sanctuary for all elderly; while they were in training for administrative positions, they were to find that a long and torturous undertaking lay ahead of them. Being young and guided by doctors Webber and Wilson, we believe they will survive and still retain their enthusiasm for elderly care.

We had become restless, after Clara was able to spend some time at her desk. The Goldsmith ladies had to return to their classes and special duties that helped pay their special fees and room and board [nbbande9].

I reported every morning to run errands and deliver Clara's special notes of encouragement that seemed to brighten the countenance of those who received them.

If the notes were of inquiry in tone, for the condition of a patient, from family, Clara always added a short note in her own handwriting.

I did inquire about the boy with a crack that showed up after a cast was removed. He had been taking his calcium every day, but not the supplement vitamin D, which allows the calcium to be absorbed more easily.

Petty, we were to find out later, had had a sore on his right hand after being contaminated by a person who had hepatitis A while helping that person work in his garden.

So doing, an act of kindness had branded Petty for life! I suspect he would never know whether a hidden virus is hiding in his liver in spite of all those Interferon shots.

Taking advantage of the mystical powers of transportation, we walked into the Lonesome Pine Café and ordered coffee, hotcakes, and eggs. We were greeted by Hap and Marion. We noticed a draft while ago (referring to my transportation) was just too busy at the time to investigate. Things around here had never slowed down the last two years. We added on enough space as a lounging area for all the elderly. It was working out fine. We had six waitresses working on that section to keep an eagle eye on those inclined to be in ill health. Just doing what little we do here had made us feel a part of the community!

The city went to the federal government for a new high-pressure water tower, tall enough to provide for a city twice this size. Ray insisted on a no-rust underground mains and proved the city could recover the cost in ten years.

The afternoon, we walked by the local newspaper and visited with the editor who was more than pleased with the economy. His circulation list had increased almost 90 percent.

My next stop was at the Farmer's Café, whose customers all seemed to be between twenty-one and thirty. Their conversation seemed to be mostly about livestock prices, cost of fodder, and price of diesel fuel. Then we were to learn that most of them had taken over their parents' work on their farms and enjoying the fellowship of parents who were not lost dog, dead dog tired all the time. That group from McCook Hospital had done a good selling the fact that rest and recreation pays off.

We talk on the phone to Chess Wilson, the farm manager for Pa Jake Smith Farms and asked if my old room was still available in the big hall. He replied, "Yeah, you left a pair of old shoes when you left. The vet and I put on masks and located them. He has been ailing ever since."

I replied, "Those were my best fishing shoes."

Chess said, "I have to hang up, the vet and I are busy helping an Arabian foal arrive here in the barn."

I said, "Yes, I see, tapping him on the shoulder."

Jumping back, he exclaimed, "Oh, you and your mystical powers of transportation!"

That night as we sat in the big hall watching the fire die down, Chess and the vet wondered how long it would take before the world knows we now have the only albino Arabian foal in the state. Someone will have to guard her around the clock. She might be stolen by morning. We sure have a problem, but Chess and the vet are very good, resourceful gentlemen. That colt could be almost a year old before the community knows about her. You can bet they have had plans A, B, C, and E- and two alternatives for each plan. Everyone knows just what he and everyone else is to do. But fate and the best of well laid plans don't always work out for everyone every time.

Chess Wilson had informed me Chet Curtis came out to help harvest every year from Topeka, Kansas. He finished four years at Manhattan and his year-extension courses dealing in grain marketing, livestock marketing, Co-op Gran MKTG, co-op farm stores rules and regulations, handling and storage at the farm site, and or the co-op local town elevator.

Chess Wilson was telling about the first year that Chet Curtis came to harvest in his truck, he had a hard time coming up with all the cash for the down payment. Valree, his little sister, was to start kindergarten that fall, almost as much as he was to start college. Valree was saving for a box of pretty pencils (crayons). Given a dollar on her birthday, she went to her little bank, retrieved the dollar, and gave it to Chet to buy a truck! He was so overwhelmed by her generosity that he promised her that when she got older, he would take her harvesting with him. Well, last harvest, he brought her out. She was just fine. She as about ten years old, asked a lot of questions, but never got in the way. Valree just about lived in that truck, went wherever Chet went. She was introduced to children near her own age who soon began riding with her. By the end of each day, they were tired little girls. The next morning, they were waiting in the truck.

One rainy morning while waiting for the weather to clear, she saw her fist snake, a huge bull that Pa Smith kept around the barn to keep down rats. She said, "That was Satan and He was almost ready to eat me." He will have to go.

Pa Smith boxed Mr. Satan and took him to a prairie-dog town grass-land that he owned ten miles away.

We stopped at the trailer that the general contractor, Mr. Ray Albertson, asked a company make for him as an office, so he could be on the location of any contract and still keep in contact; the trailer had gone with him every summer. His wife had reminded him, just two years ago, what a wonderful time they had in a small town near the Kansas, Colorado, border. After the children had started to school, he made Omaha headquarters for his company. He bought a huge home thinking that the Albertson family was settled in for life. Already, Ray was becoming less restless. His son, Joe, had become very proficient in leading the company through several year of profit.

Ray wandered into the drafting rooms and asked for the plan of the formal gardens. Asking how near the head gardner had come to the original lay-out model, he was told almost to every single flower.

"Sir, this will match any formal garden in England."

Joe said the other day the head of garden maintained I will be inexpensive to maintain, which, looking down the years, needed to be kept in mind. A garden is like a child, it needs tender loving care every day!

Ray's wife, Evelan, had been staying at the combo office-home almost since the ground had been broken for the Paradise Village apartments. As they were quite nearing completion, the two returned to Omaha for what turned out to be weeks of horrifying, nerve-shredding anxiety just looking through memorabilia.

A kind neighbor lady came calling one afternoon and found a very forlorn Ray sitting in a chair that was a gift from Evelan and their two sons on his fifth [nbbande10] birthday. Evelan, sitting on an old lounge that had belonged to her grandmother, was sobbing as though her heart had been broken.

The kindly neighbor lady was aghast. "Why are you all weeping amidst all this treasure?" she asked. "Every single piece needs to be in a museum!"

"That is the solution on our problem!" shouted Ray and probably for many others who were moving into the apartments!

"I shall talk to Joe and our accountants when we go back. I am sure there must be some tax breaks in this deal; that should please everyone.

"We can build alcoves according to the size of each exhibit.

I shall trot down to the main office," Ray said as he reached for the car keys.

We have seen another side of elderly dependency that can creep up on a person who has been active most of his or her life…

In the twinkling of an eye, an idea was born in Ray's mind. This would keep Ray and Evelan on a smooth and congenial relationship as they traveled the pre-elderly and the elderly pathway of life.

We hope to hear more of this family. Remember, their son, Jim, is just finishing his freshman year of college. Somehow, somewhere in our narrative, we are shown he is the more sensitive of the two sons.

We hope to hear more about the museum later in this narrative.

Ray Albertson called Joe from the main office in Omaha after talking to his office staff and looking through various plans of buildings the company had built for other uses, thinking it would save some time if the outer shell could be adapted alcove designs for each exhibit.

He then asked the head of the model-building department to gather all information on the qualifications of a good general manager, one who would be capable of selecting staff capable of recognizing antique material and ability to display it safely.

If one had a particular room in his or her home-stead where he or she had spend many happy hours, his or her alcove should reflect that, along with pictures on the walls of departed parents, grandparents, etc.

Should tragedy strike either of a couple, just think how comforting it could be (accompanied by favorite caring nurses (In earlier pages, we talked about those skilled angels of mercy who would be assigned to the near elderly and the elderly, as we felt those two stages of aging are perhaps the most dependent stages of life, perhaps even more than early childhood, to which they are sometimes compared).

We have seen on this page and the preceding ones that Ray had began to slow his paces in life, and the museum burden was apt to fall on Joe's shoulders. We have no doubt that Joe will complete his tasks in life just as his father had done all of his adult life. Of it all, this just a page, a small incident in the life of Ray and Evelan; we must return to Paradise Village, because the seventh floor apartments are ready for occupancy!

We ate breakfast the next morning at the Lonesome Pine Café, Paradise village (zip code a few years in the future), and walked a few blocks to the local newspaper office. We concluded no one knew about the new construction being planned, saying nothing about the trip to Omaha. We did learn that the whole town was bussing about the whole building. To my way of thinking, those questions were legitimate questions that should be cleared up, or the feelings of the whole town will be hurt beyond repair a situation that had happened to Ray early in his career and one he never let happen again!

Not being any too skilled at PR myself, we talked to Joe, who called a conformance of the three wives of the auto salesmen who had been the backbone of PR without really realizing their talent.

Joe also called in all the subcontractors and their foremen, wanting to know if everything they had installed had been checked and working properly. Going over a long list, he asked that all of the elevators be rechecked by reliable journeymen who would operate them all day on a two-day open-house. The same would be done for every item in the building! Then he called the group who had the contract for the operation of the cafeteria to prepare a light balanced meal for everyone who visited the cafeteria. After a thorough cleaning of the building, we shall get everyone moved into their suite and as soon as everyone is comfortable, it might be some time before the residents will want to do anything but relax and enjoy their new surroundings.

The nurses who were to be assigned the elderly in their assisted living situation had been trained to watch their clients for signs of discontent due to feelings of inadequacy in not doing various tasks themselves as they used to do when they were much younger. They must be made to realize they would tax their strength enough to cause a feeling become physical discomfort.

We have a feeling this will not begin to reveal itself until they have had a month of relaxation[nbbande11]. We hope this can be avoided by a lively dance band that brings them to the floor before switching to slow, dreamy music with frequent rest periods for conversation.

We know that keeping such a large group of elderly people entertained and in good health will be a huge strain on those in the entertainment communities.

Joe Albertson contacted the PR ladies and their auto-salesmen, asking them to a lunch at the Lonesome Pine Café on a rather short notice and asked them to have their notebooks for a hush-hush-rush-rush situation and that might have to work later than usual. He then called the Lonesome Pine and made reservations for lunch for at least eight in the private conference room, and repeated hush-hush-rush-rush caution to Hap and Marion.

Joe then sat down and outlined wheat he intended to say at the conference. When he had finished, he read the list over. He then leaned back and called his father in Omaha, informing him of his oversight and what he intended to do about it. His father's only comment was "I am proud of you, son!"

Joe stopped by the newspaper office to speak to the editor who happened to be in a deep discussion with the mayor. On seeing Joe enter the doorway, their faces brightened and they both chorused, "Are you planning to have an open house?"

Joe's face broke into a big grin. "Yes, yes, but I need some advice!" How about coming to lunch at the Lonesome Pine where I have asked most of my personnel to meet me in the conference room in about ten minutes?"

"A free lunch! And our choice from the menu! Are you ready to ride? Pile in the oldest auto parked in front. Time nor tired waits for no man!"

Arriving at the Lonesome Pine Café, the tyro were seated, their orders taken and be brought with the others, who had ordered as they arrived...."

Taking the gavel that had been placed near his plate, Joe called for attention and began to speak.

In jubilation of the completing the huge construction contract, we must remember everyone in Paradise Village and-I mean everyone- has encouraged and assisted in its completion with their enthusiasm and expertise.

"It is fitting that they should be the first to share in the newness and freshness of the jewels created in Paradise Village.

"We have been assured that everything has been installed correctly and in working order. All the sub-contractors have assured me they will have all their personnel on hand to demonstrate and operate everything for a week. After that, they have provided our maintenance supervisors with enough books of instructions (continued on page 102) to allow each maintenance employee a set of books for home study to keep current. There are books that tell where to look for the trouble if certain conditions are causing down time."

Joe continued.

"Every subcontractor has told me they want to point with pride to our sales personnel and future consumers that good equipment that is well maintained is an economically sound investment.

"Having related all this well-founded information, what is my dilemma you asked? It is that we have less than a week to plan and execute a two-day open-house that the city and county so rightly deserve.

"Can we do it and not appear unprofessional? May I suggest we flood the city and county with advertising in tomorrow's morning mail, making sure it is understood the apartments will not be occupied until after the open house? Can that be done?

"The kitchen will be somewhat out of bounds as they will serve several choices of good dietary meals all day both days. Be sure everyone receives recognition for his or her efforts.

"You, public relations, should recognize that the mere mention of the free meals for two days will destroy a large portion of the income of our two local eating establishments and could destroy our reputation as considerate, understanding personnel in the community. That was not my intention," continued Joe. "We wanted to show the public how we will be entertaining their elderly loved ones who would come to live at Paradise Gardens. This meeting is now open for discussion, our editor has a deadline to make!"

The P.R. group began writing the flyers that were to go out the next morning, announcing the open-house. These were to state the days, dates, and the door-opening hour of 8:00 AM and closing time of 6:00 PM "Bring well marked bed-sheets and pillow cases, we will do them for you!" The rest of the full-page ad described all the attributes of the retirement living at the Paradise Gardens Apartments, including a booklet that described everything in the building and its use for the care of the elderly.

After the morning paper was delivered, the phones began to ring in Joe's office from people wanting to know if they could bring all their laundry! Just as he had anticipated. He explained he wanted everyone to see how fast and efficient the new machines were, to relive the elderly of burdensome tasks. Many called just to say the ad was unique and that they were planning to tour the building.

The editor had half a column telling the people in the rural communities this was a wonderful opportunity to see how much thought and care had been incorporated for the care of the elderly and invited them to view a picture hanging in his office of an indigent country farm of a century ago, and pledged that his reporters would be writing about every phase of the open-house.

The mayor pledged to have forces out in their new uniforms directing traffic in and out of the huge parking lot.

The morning of September 1 of the year 2000, the sun pushed the milk-white clouds aside, disclosing the clear blue sky about the huge complex of the Paradise Garden, which had been just a dream of young John Smith and his bride. They began to realize the thousands of people from all walks of life that dedicated themselves and their expertise it had taken to bring this phase of their lives to bring health and happiness to the elderly.

Glancing at his watch, he said, "This is a dry-run open-house day. In an hour, the doors will open and everyone will see how we plan to accomplish our dreams."

John and Erma progressed rapidly in their classes after their probation year, he as a medical doctor and administrator and Erma as the director of nursing. They had graduated with honors even while working part time in McCook Hospital to help with the expense.

His office was quite large, in the north side of the row of the seventh floor apartments, where he could look south to the self-standing intensive care unit.

He and Erma had promised that they would make an inspection trip through that building every morning and spend a little time with each patient, making sure that they are not forgotten and received the best attention until they were able to return to their own apartments. He would say to each, "Do not ever lose hope."

There was a chapel arranged for wheelchairs. An order went that if a patient asked to go to the chapel, take them, regardless of UV stand, oxygen tank, etc. Always, the nurse was to stand by should an emergency arise.

The intensive care unit was equipped with all-new equipment, donated by the estate of a rancher who had asked, on his death-bed, to remain anonymous.

John Smith, in the course of his schooling, had met many competent young doctors, some of whom had shown great compassion for the elderly. There were some who were very competent with the x-ray as a diagnostic tool. He and Erma had invited them all to an inspection tour of the four-story medical office and laboratory building just two hundred feet south of the ICU building, connected by a wide Plexiglas-covered walkway. North of the doctors' office and lab building was the helicopter emergency landing. When John Smith contemplated all these, he wondered how many state and federal agencies Joe Albertson had to contend with, and made sure everyone in the emergency operation was properly licensed. The Albertson home office- Omaha had, with the assistance of the suppliers of the equipment in the ICU and the laboratory, a booklet that contained the name and number of every piece and name of the personnel who installed the equipment. (This information may sound trivial. Just try talking to a garage service man ten blocks from your home. He will want to know the make of your car, license number, where it is located (in your garage, in the drive, in front of the house, house number, are all the tires flat, will someone be there with the auto key (never leave your house key on the auto key-ring (It has been done, they will tell you); also, your phone number in case you forgot to say what street you live on!

By the time the open-house for the apartments was over, the debris would all be sorted for the things that could be recycled and placed in the huge, marked containers that the trash-haul contractor was to remove and replace every day. It had been anticipated that when all the apartments were occupied, several of each type of container would be needed. These containers would be placed in a large fenced and paved lot with the contractors personnel in attendance to assist in loading and unloading and in keeping the whole lot clear of debris in containers and that there was a complete turnover of containers emptied every day.

The two-day house would give each floor manager time to estimate the amount of trash their floor would have to contend with each day.

All trash would be picked up from a tilt-out container in the hole of the kitchen wall using color-coded plastic bags red for fresh garbage, blue for plastic materials, green for glass, yellow for tin cans, and black for newspapers. All would be picked up by special security personnel using special electricity—powered trucks with demountable box-beds traveling through a special Plexiglas—covered run-way to the trash containers. Each of the seven floors was to be worked at least twice a week and the holes power-vacuumed every day except on weekends.

Ray Albertson, Joe, and members of their home office-Omaha humbled themselves and went asking for advice before buying and having anything in the ICU and the doctors' office building, saying, "This is something that is beyond our expertise, will you help and advise us on these two buildings?"

Everyone realized this was the focal point of the whole operation the alpha and omega.

John and Erma Smith's offices, located at the east end of the seventh floor of the apartments, extended westward along either side of the very wide hall. On either end of the long wide hall were large freight elevators that extended to the basement. The east elevator would be used by those who were moving into the apartments, although either could be used…. However, the west freight elevator was primarily to be used by the kitchen detail.

The kitchen was deemed potentially less quiet because of the presence of good mixers, grinders, pans, and roasting pans, etc.

After preparation, the food was to be placed in portable hand-guided electric warming cabinets that could be plugged into the electric system, both in the kitchen and the cafeteria.

The kitchen, located along the north wall of the basement, had been designed and laid out by the home office drafting department to eliminate handling of heavy roasting and baking pans whenever large quantities were required.

Because of the kitchen location, a special draft-hood was placed over every stove and oven and vented through a disposable filter, to be changed every twenty-four hours. It had been estimated that with the three-foot diameter stainless steel tube over eight stories tall, the atmospheric pressure (14 lb per square inch) could be overcome by a relatively large exhaust fan that would draft the grease to the filter but no further, and eliminate a grease fire in the tube, top end to be covered with a conical rain-cap would extend about one foot below the top of the exhaust tube. Because of the height, a required red light, proper lighting, and grounding protection were required.

Using the washers and dryers in the first six apartments, the housekeeping department washed, dried, and folded 1000 pair of sheets and pillowcases, all tagged with the names, addresses, and phone numbers on a plastic memory tag with the date and year of the one who brought them in. The second day, the numbers were about the same.

The public relations people had estimated that there might be as many meals for 1000 people in the crowded cafeteria most of the day. They ate quickly, eager to meet the next tour-guide through the apartments of the formal gardens.

The news-media and television lavished with praise the thoughtfulness of the personnel in the handling the huge crowds considering the long lines never seemed to stop moving.

The cleaning up, which required one day, concentrated on the apartments to the tenants could start moving in.

The tenants were cautioned not to move too much until after they have lived in smaller quarters a week or so, and to bring in the things they miss the most. They were provided a guide list to select the number of items most people use most often. Many brought their favorite lounge-chairs, electric reading lamps, a china cabinet, their best china, best silver, set of stainless (for everyday, which will end up as once in a while!).

There had been many books donated for a library on the sixth floor. These would, of necessity, need sorting, cataloging, and shelving.

This could be put off until some group need a rainy day job!

While in school, John Smith found a person that he felt had many of the qualifications to be administrator of the ICU. The person was among his group of young medical friends. John asked him to mail a resume; having read the resume, John Smith mailed a formal invitation of Doctor W. Grover and his wife to dinner and investigate the ICU before it is ever open to the public.

In the intern, John and Erma-along with the local media-escorted all the residents on the seventh floor and their adult children through the ICU as they were, because of their age, the most likely to require that type of care in the ensuing year. John and Erma were of the mind that first hand, credible knowledge could soothe the against about improper physical treatment of the elderly; that what one so often hears from someone calling a situation neglect is in reality a judgment call by a harried, over-tired aid who had to leave a patient in a mess to assist a patient who had loosed his or her restraints and fallen out of bed and perhaps broken bones.

In the opinion of the author, restraints should never be used on an elderly person as a form of punishment for an infraction; keep in mind tether restraints and safety bed rail are two different classifications. The tether, to my knowledge is not used in care-homes in our modern times, as it looks demeaning to the beholder's eye.

The bed-tail, in place, means we care to place this just as a reminder that one is in a high bed and might fall. Just turn on the light, we will come.

Dr. W. Grover and his wife, Eloise, accepted the invitation to dine. They were shown the ICU just two days before the dead-line on the opening day of October.

Once again, the PR groups came to the rescue. They were attending a card party at the Smiths when they overheard Eloise say, rather sharply, "Will, where in this world will we ever find a place as mice as where we are now?"

Drawing her husband aside, Lily Andrew asked in a rather conspiratory voice, "Please, take Dr. Will to play gold tomorrow place... I am going to show Eloise that new farm house (a Southern Cross ranch in miniature.) We should help; John really needs this doctor.

We know that Eloise talks about her horses and her background as a farm-girl. Don't you worry, we are not about to let Dr. Will be the play-boy and Dr. John do all the work!"

Mr. Andrew and Dr. Will Grover played golf the next day. Dr. Will did not play well, seemingly to be in a daze at times, with moments of not being able to make a decision quickly. They quit and went back to town where they were taken to the old family doctor on main street, it being the nearest. After he listened to the vitals, he called Dr. John Smith and told him he thought his friend might be having a stroke. He then asked if ICU was open enough to run some tests. That was how Dr. Will became the first patient in the new ICU. It was also how Dr. Annatta Quinn was sent from McCook hospital. She was a charming and skilled physician who organized her office, interviewed her nurse, office manager with knowledge of keeping detailed records. She was not sharp tongued but she was always in control.

It was also understood that Dr. Quinn was appointed to the position of the administrator of the entire ICU and a contract was drawn up and signed. This particular action may, at first reading, seem careless, were it not for the peculiar circumstance causing Mr. Will Grover's stroke.

One might pause here and observe that John Smith had not completely gained his ability to judge character. However, John may have let his friendship with Dr. Grover influence his judgment of his friend's ability and character.

A few pages back, Joe Albertson, almost created a disaster for himself and for his father; it would have been more costly had he not humbled himself and asked advice from his staff and the editor. Remember how everyone pitched in to help him save his oversight of the open house? Same situation, only John's could have disrupted a lot more lives.

John Smith, in his situation, may have to look over his shoulder for several years before he is free from doubt in his own mind if his decision was correct! We shall wish him well and hope he realizes dreams are just dreams until one puts them to work!

In the ensuing months, the ICU, under the supervision of Dr. Annatta Quinn, was beginning to become a very well-organized part of the whole system.

The ICU has now been in operation under the supervision of Ms. Annatta Quinn over three months. There was a rush after the open-house to make sure everyone received their flu and pneumonia shots. Every-one including doctors, their families, all the nurses, technicians, food-handlers, and groundskeepers received shots.

Then the mayor and the county commissioners called on John Smith, asking if they might receive the shots also, at the city and county expense, of course. John's reply was that any-one running a fever must not receive the shots until the fever had subsided and one had been checked by a doctor. That statement seemed to sound like a good judgment to the group. John Smith handed out a medical statement about flu. He said there were many types of flu and that it was impossible to know which type would appear first, and, by that time, it would be too late for the medical laboratory to determine the type and make a safe vaccine that will be not too virulent or too mild, because it sometimes takes weeks of failed cultures to produce a formula, then test and approved. Those living in towns, cities, and farms may require a different formula from those living in more secluded areas. However, those living in apartment buildings should have the shots as there's more chance of the virus spreading because of the weaker immune system of the elderly.

Dr. Annatta Quinn had been studying the chart and blood test ordered each of the four-shift nurses (Yes, she had put the four-shift system, just as they had a McCook Hospital). The tests were all drawn just before the shift change. Then she asked another nurse to make the same draw right after Dr. Will

Grover received a visitor; to record his name and appearance and to drop the record in her personal mail slot after recording it on the computer; then called the lab and asked for a special report on Dr. Will Grover's blood test sent to her, and to save the slides and flood samples, if possible before the results of the last test were recorded in the computer. Having completed her task, she rubbed her eyes as a tear rolled down her cheek.

She had known Dr. Grover since he was a teenager. She hoped that she was just chasing a ghost. She had been a teacher of a class in a small church in her youth, and Will Grover was a bright, attentive student, always looking forward to the time when he could start to college and a good medical school—and now this is terrible stroke—just at the start of his career. And so far, all her skills and knowledge and the group from McCook she had called in were unable to agree on a probable cause. Well, it would take another week before the last tests results were known. Turning to her office nurse, she said, "Please call x-ray and asked for another complete spinal. We know that the man had been playing golf and drives hard. He may have twisted the spine in several places. I thought I detected several places along the spine this morning in the neck and shoulder areas.

"Between the first and second x-rays, warm packs were to be placed and the heat to be increased a little until the patient is sweating. Be careful not to blister the skin; that should relax the tissue and help relieve the pressure on any nerve.

"If we find nothing," Dr. Quinn continued, "we should try another MRI from a different angle, looking for any pressure on the spinal column. I don't feel we have much time left, because nerve tissue deteriorates rather quickly. Let's hope we are not too late." It will take about a week before all the tests and records are dropped into the mall slot in her office door.

In the meantime, all thirty-six apartments on the north side of the seventh floor and the thirty-six apartments on the south side of the seventh floor were moving in as fast as the east and west freight elevators (with the regular operator and two temporary helpers) could make a trip down and back. It was understood the west freight elevator was reserved primarily for building maintenance and good handling.

It was hoped the fifth and fourth floors would be fully occupied the next month, the weather staying favorable. There had been no grouching from the residents, attributed to the trained nurses who had been assigned to assist in adjusting to the relaxing style of apartment living.

Their jobs gave the nurses knowledge of the personalities of the people under their care. To state it another way, they were like a caring, well-adjusted daughter.

Ray Albertson and his wife had moved into one of the large apartments on the north side, just to the west of John and Erma, whose living quarters were small compared to the others on the north side, both their offices occupying the floor space of four of the largest apartments. They both had started with five clerks and an office manager, and soon added five more clerks.

The computer system allowed John to be in touch with every department in the whole complex. He and Erma made it in a practice to visit the ICU every morning.

This morning, they visited the chapel. They then strolled over to see Dr. Will Grover to read his chart, and also Dr. Annatta Quinn, who was almost in tears again.

"I don't want to lose the first patient in this facility!" she wailed.

"We don't, either!" exclaimed John and Erma in unison, "but we know death is an ultimate event that only God has the ability to control. We humans have the ability to prolong life. We must do, with our talents, nothing to destroy life."

Dr. Annatta Quinn went over everything she and her group of nurses had done for the patient, including the MRI, taken with the patient lying on his side.

Dr. John Smith then asked if his friend had been able to speak at any time since his arrival. When told that Dr. Will Grover was incoherent since his admittance. Dr. John Smith asked to hear all the tapes, starting from day one. In the office of Dr. Annatta Quinn, the three listened to the tapes; Erma had it played more slowly. I heard a lot of Latin in there, but it was playing so fast… ," her voice trailed off as she glanced the face of John.

Turning to Dr. Quinn, John said softly, "Call x-ray and asked for a frontal lobe of your MRI as well. We are looking for a clot of a tumor or anything that's causing pressure. Have them call when ready. In the meantime, we shall listen to the rest of the tapes. There might be more valuable information on those tapes!"

John and Erma listened to the tapes played slowly, as the words in Latin merged from the tape, stopping and starting and sometimes playing a word of phrase over several times until they both agreed on the meaning. The word in Latin, "head-ache" was repeated many times as were the words "back" and "spine" that the man was in great pain and hallucinating.

At this time, John called the lab to test all blood samples from Dr. Will Grover for any medication or substance known to cause hallucination.

John and Erma continued to monitor the tapes. Proper names began to appear as the tape (the time on the tape showing near the end of the afternoon shift and twice, shortly after the start of the start of the next). The names John and Erma had never heard of; perhaps they were Asian. John turned to Erma with fear in his eyes.

"We are wasting valuable time. I know a detective in McCook that specializes in drugs. He has his own plane. He could be here in a matter of two or three hours if he isn't on a case."

Reaching for the phone, he dialed the number and in moments, he was speaking Mr. Don McCarthy, who assured John he would be there in two hours and minutes.

"Good, I shall have our security people meet you at our airport. We shall have a steak dinner waiting in our apartment, over and out!"

This would be the first real meal John and Erma were to eat in their apartment. Until now, they had eaten in the staff's dining room, becoming acquainted with any problem that might have arisen that day and usually clearing them up quickly.

It was somewhat troubling to think that this was not the romantic dinner Erma had dreamed of while they were still in school.

John had called the manager of the cafeteria, who came to the private office of Dr. Annatta Quinn. John explained they were having unexpected overnight guests and dinner at eight thirty that evening.

The manager made careful notes and said, "We have some special dishes and silver-ware with the Paradise Garden logo. You won't have any dishes to wash. I understand you have a standing order that there is to be no alcoholic drinks. I shall send out our most skilled serving staff. Your house staff, of course, should be near to let us in at seven thirty. We all know tonight is the first dinner since you moved into your apartment, and we know you have a perfect right to have a case of the jitters. We all wish you an enjoyable evening. One of the waitress will take some photos, but not without your permission. It will be her pleasure and mine."

Calling his assistants who placed the information on the computer, he assigned selection of the choice steaks and sauces to the chefs, saying, "We have less than three hours to have it on the table. These are the occasions we specialize in. This is all to be served out of the Smith kitchen. Someone will go ahead with the dishes and silverware (We wonder if the assistant isn't slightly rattled by the time schedule?).

Although it was well-organized, we were not privy to the secrecy of the dinner that night, nor of the meeting that followed. That day, we asked if we would sit with an elderly widow who was suffering from malnutrition and de-hydration and was so restless she was pulling the needles from her arms. It would be several weeks before we heard, second hand, of course, just what de-tective Don McCarthy had determined was causing Dr. Grover's problem.

We walked into Minie Olesons room in the ICU that morning. She lay still exhausted and gaunt; her hair, now in a long braid, which was once golden blond, was now a pale whitish gray, Depression and despair molded her face where the blush of red rose should have been,

We talked a few moments and exchanged a few pleasantries about the old days. She asked, "Why did you always leave the bridle on that poor pony you rode to school? That horse had to drink with the ugly iron bit in its mouth and eat that ear of corn you gave him at noon, too."

We said, "Minie… I was not tall enough to take that bridle off! If I did, I could not put it back on because he always held his head out of my reach! My father and his neighbors built a pole barn, open to the south, with the log hitch rail four feet inside from the north wall. There was a door in the east and west wall, so who-ever mowed the school yard could store the cuttings in that nar-row space so the horses could reach the hay!"

By that time, it was lunch time.

A nutritious, warm broth in a clear plastic, two-handled cup and another with orange juice were brought in. My coffee was in an insulated cup that also had two handles. We noticed that Minie Oleson had not picked up her cup. I said with a comic flourish, "Ms. Oleson, may I present you with your morning ambrosia?"

She smiled weakly and reached for the cup. Making sure she had a firm grip, I turned the cup and she took and finished the broth. Between deep breaths, she said, "I am ready for the juice and then I shall take a nap."

Just as she drifted off to sleep, Marge, the beautician, came by with her note pad. We told her how Ms. Oleson had such beautiful golden hair The braid around her hair was like a halo and her pale pink cheeks were like a blushing rose.

Marge continued her writing, then laid down her notes and said to me, "I have made a note to call Dr. Quinn and asked her when she thinks Ms. Oleson will be strong enough to have a facial and shampoo, to call me and I shall work her into the schedule, and a nurse can bring her over to the shop. I always say, "If felling depressed, have your hair done and a facial!"

Ms. Oleson began eating soft foods the second day we visited, but Dr. Quinn thought the extra boost of vitamins from the intravenous needles was necessary for the long drain on her body cause by her poor diet.

We visited Ms. Oleson every day for a week before she began to feel better and her outlook about her life began to change for the better. He had walked with me in the halls of the hospital without the two nurses several days by now when the call came through Dr. Annatta Quinn that Ms. Oleson had an appointment with the hairdresser at two PM that day. She cut our walk short that day and rushed back to her room, where a waiting nurse waved a hand at me, saying, "Bye bye, this lady is to have a warm bath and then a cool rub-down. I have some rose soap flakes for the bath and some rose cream for the rub-down."

Needless to say, picking up my lunch, I wandered about, looking for a place to sit down. I came upon a small room with six tables that we had never noticed before, poured myself a cup of coffee from the fancy coffee-maker, and sat down at a table in the far corner. I was about half way finished with my lunch when in walked two doctors, their trays with only tuna sandwich and an empty cup. *Must have had a hearty breakfast*, I thought.

The two *doctors* (?) drew cups of hot water from the coffee-maker and sat down. One produced a tea-bag, swirled it around in his cup, then handed it to his partner! He then started talking about Dr. Grover.

I started making notes! I could not hear their names, I but could hear their brogue and see the sallow skin and rough clothing under their white coats. I hoped I could gather enough information that would help Dr. Will Grover, when I heard one say, "Were dishes and the tea-bag! Just then, a security man walked in!

We called "Mayday! Mayday! Stop those men!"

The security man quickly shut the door with his foot as he drew his gun and advanced to within ten feet of the two tea-guzzlers.

"Why are you in this private lunchroom?"

"We thought this was the doctors' lounge. We meant no harm!"

At that very moment, Detective Don McCarthy came in, followed by six security personnel. He explained to the two men they had been observed on camera in Dr. Will Grover's hospital room and had watched them serve what appeared to be a tea-bag, into a cup of warm water. They watched as he raised the cup to his lips.

"Now, we find you two with your finger-prints all over the dishes and the residue of a substance that will compare with what was found in Dr. Will Grover's cup."

The two guilty men were charged and held in the county jail with a huge bail bond that neither they nor their syndicate was able to raise. It would be many weeks before the case came to trail.

We might say here that no one in the Smith family believed in the death penalty. Yet, these two men had deliberately tried to destroy a man's life. A friend who had great potential for the welfare of all humanity had been reduced to less than half of his physical capabilities—for what? We wish we could look into the future with some reliability, but we cannot, of course.

His good wife, Eloise, had visited Will every day and in the ensuing weeks, she realized her husband would require a lot of physical therapy.

Between then, they decided they should keep the farm (the Southern Cross ranch in miniature).

We shall not go into great detail at this time about their ranch, first to avoid confusion with the working Ranch Bar Z of the Goldsmiths and the fact that Eloise had plans in mind for some changes, like ramps to replace the outside step elevators from the basement to their rooms. They also considered the possibility of taking in some youths with disabilities, to change their names to something like Sunshine, Happiness, Health.

Which one Joe Albertson will give priority-Sunshine Ranch or the museum for his father?

With the two drug dealers safely locked up, the stress through the ICU subsided quickly under Dr. Annatta Quinn's skillful management of the department.

Several elderly people were brought in from the sixth floor. They were those who were finding sudden change from their home to the smaller quarters of the apartments hard and had not adjusted well to the diets. They were brought to the ICU with their regular nurses. Under Ms. Quinn's management and insight, she discovered that the nurses were too overzealous with their assistance in the routine of daily living, which became cause of irritation to the elderly people, which over time could cause them to complain of physical ailments and if prolonged, destroy their health.

These nurses had been trained to be on the lookout for this type of situation and now know firsthand the results; thus, they made a vow that the same situation would be remembered. The next year, they won the first, second, and third prizes for their adherence to rules with no violations.

It has been over two years since the day The Cooperative Paradise Village Apartments and Medical Care Complex were completed.

The association had held their second annual meeting. Chet Curtis, after finishing college, had become a member of the community and taken an apartment on the ground floor, where a huge office had been constructed for him because he had been elected general manager of the co-op family general store (food, general merchandize, dry goods, and clothing) when the other manager tired, and also that of the co-op apartments.

That is a big load for a young man just out college. He, like his sister, asked a lot of questions all his life. We are sure their lives will be most pleasant, because they both had the habit of wearing a very tight hat band in their interactions with the public.

The End.